THE
MIND TEST

THE MIND TEST

by Rita Aero and Elliot Weiner, Ph.D.

WILLIAM MORROW AND COMPANY, INC.
New York, 1981

ACKNOWLEDGMENTS

The authors wish to express their gratitude to Howard Rheingold for his contributions to the text; to Barbara Stewart, Ph.D., for her valuable suggestions and advice; and to Laura Drake for her help with the initial research. We are also indebted to Rosalie Brandon and David Malcolm for their support during the execution of this project, and to Stephanie Rick for her assistance with the book's design. We are particularly grateful to the psychologists, psychiatrists, and social workers who allowed us to reprint the tests that they developed, and to our editor, James Landis, for his encouragement and support.

Library of Congress Cataloging-in-Publication Data

Aero, Rita.
  The mind test.

  "Morrow Quill paperbacks."

  Bibliography: p.
  1. Psychological tests. I. Weiner, Elliott A. II. Title.
BF176.A43   155.2'8   81-2341
ISBN 0-688-00401-6 (pbk.)   AACR2

Printed in the United States of America

19 20

BOOK DESIGN BY RITA AERO

Contents

A Note to the Reader   6

How to Use This Book   7

The Mind Test   8
     by ELLIOT A. WEINER AND RITA AERO

Chapter One   Personality Analysis

Social Desirability Scale   17
by DOUGLAS P. CROWNE and DAVID MARLOWE

Locus of Control Scale   20
by STEPHEN NOWICKI, JR., and B. STRICKLAND

Self-Acceptance Scale   24
by EMANUEL M. BERGER

Change Seeker Index   28
by WARREN K. GARLINGTON and HELEN E. SHIMOTA

Self-Image Checklist   35
by ELLIOT A. WEINER

Fear of Appearing Incompetent Scale   38
by LAWRENCE R. GOOD and KATHERINE C. GOOD

Chapter Two   Stress

Life Change Index Scale   45
by THOMAS HOLMES

The Annoyance List   47

Physical Anxiety Questionnaire   49
by LAWRENCE R. GOOD and CHESTER C. PARKER

Stress Quiz   51

Chapter Three   Anxiety

Fear of Negative Evaluation Scale   57
by DAVID WATSON and RONALD FRIEND

Hostility Inventory   60
by ARNOLD H. BUSS and ANN DURKEE

Self-Consciousness Scale   67
by ALLAN FENIGSTEIN, MICHAEL SCHEIER, and ARNOLD BUSS

Moral Anxiety Questionnaire   70
by LAWRENCE R. GOOD and KATHERINE C. GOOD

Death Concern Scale   72
by LOUIS S. DICKSTEIN

Chapter Four **Fear**

Fear Survey Schedule II
by JAMES H. GEER   79

Dental Anxiety Scale
by NORMAN L. CORAH   82

Anxiety Questionnaires
by PETER J. LANG   84

Reducer-Augmenter Scale
by ALAN VANDO   92

Chapter Five **Marital & Family Relationships**

Marital Adjustment Test
by HARVEY J. LOCKE and KARL M. WALLACE   101

Index of Family Relations
by WALTER W. HUDSON   103

Marital Role Decisions Questionnaire
by JOSEPH E. GRUSH and JANET G. YEHL   107

Index of Sexual Satisfaction
by WALTER W. HUDSON   115

Chapter Six **Depression**

Beck Depression Inventory
by AARON T. BECK   121

Desire for Novelty Scale
by PAMELA H. PEARSON   126

Self-Rating Depression Scale
by WILLIAM K. ZUNG   128

Generalized Contentment Scale
by WALTER W. HUDSON   131

Chapter Seven **Vocation**

Interest Check List
by THE UNITED STATES DEPARTMENT OF LABOR   137

Telic Dominance Scale
by STEPHEN MURGATROYD, CYRIL RUSHTON, MICHALE APTER, and COLETTE RAY   142

Job Satisfaction Index
by BPC PUBLISHING LTD.   146

The Quick Job-Hunting Map: The Party
by RICHARD N. BOLLES   151

Chapter Eight **Interpersonal Relationships**

Acceptance of Others Scale
by WILLIAM F. FEY
157

Social Interest Scale
by JAMES E. CRANDALL
160

Index of Peer Relations
by WALTER W. HUDSON
163

Assertion Questionnaire
by PETER LEWINSOHN
166

APPENDICES

Selecting a Therapist
171

Information About Available Services
171

Attitudes Toward Seeking Professional Psychological Help Scale
by EDWARD H. FISCHER and JOHN L. TURNER
173

A Note to the Reader

*O*ver 2,500 psychological tests are in use in the United States today. If you were educated and are employed in this country, then you have been exposed to one or more of them—and chances are you have never seen the results.

Psychological tests are the tools of mental health professionals—psychologists, sociologists, and psychiatrists. In the past ten years, with the emergence of sophisticated computer technologies, the field of testing has gained in importance and efficacy. Many such tests, because they are accessible and standardized, are now routinely used by educators and employers as well as by the military and market researchers. These institutions use psychological tests to find out whether we will fit into an organization, what kinds of products we are likely to buy, what skills and aptitudes we have that may be valuable to the testing organization. The psyche of the individual American is continually probed, measured, and analyzed by those who require such information.

In this book you will find a number of these tests along with instructions so that you may take them yourself and analyze your own scores. You may not want to take all the tests but only those that are of special interest to you. To help pinpoint those areas we've included a master test, the Mind Test, which begins on the following page.

How to Use This Book

*T*he book is arranged into eight chapters, each dealing with a different area of psychological concern. At one time or another most of us are faced with a particular sensitivity to any one of these areas—whether it is the stress that comes from an intense life-style, the difficulties that arise in relationships with loved ones, or the anxiety that comes when looking for the right job. Sometimes, though, we may feel an unease, a dissatisfaction, or a need to change that is too subtle to pinpoint as a specific personality concern.

To help clarify your feelings and to make this book a more effective tool, we have included a test on the next page, the Mind Test, for you to take. The Mind Test will help you discover to what extent each of the eight areas of concern is affecting your life right now, and will provide you with a personal path through the book. After taking and scoring the Mind Test, you will have some idea of which chapter to begin with, and an order of importance that each chapter has in your life.

In using these tests to mirror your own psyche, you will catch a unique glimpse of your psychological makeup. Whether you're looking at your marriage, your job satisfaction, or your levels of assertiveness or stress, you are likely to discover something new about yourself or about the ways you relate to others and the way that others see you.

It's best to take the test now. When you turn the page you will find the beginning of the Mind Test and an answer sheet. Tear out the answer sheet (there are extra copies in the back of the book) and begin the test. Answer all 120 true-false questions.

The Mind Test

by Elliot A. Weiner
and Rita Aero

Below are 120 statements. Read each one and decide whether that statement is true (T) or false (F) as it pertains to you. Blacken the appropriate box on the answer sheet provided. When you have answered all of the questions, see page 13 for scoring instructions.

---

1. I know pretty much what I want out of life.
2. I live or work in a noisy area.
3. Lately I feel nervous or anxious more often than I would like to.
4. I have recurrent dreams that wake me up during the night.
5. The family in which I was raised was a happy one.
6. I am often full of energy.
7. I am definitely underpaid at work for the job I do.
8. I often regret what I say to others.
9. When I finish a job, I am never completely satisfied with the results.
10. I seldom worry about money matters.
11. Taking this test is making me nervous.
12. I have certain fears that make me physically upset.
13. Lately I think about having sexual contact with someone other than my partner.
14. I am as happy as most people I know.
15. I'm not really interested in the work that I do.
16. People often act as if they don't care about me.
17. I'd rather spend my time with other people than be alone.
18. I have taken out or applied for a loan during the past year.
19. I am not sure if I am fulfilling all of my responsibilities.
20. I usually get very nervous when I walk down a dark street by myself.
21. Most members of my family don't really know me.
22. I sometimes don't seem to care what happens.
23. My supervisor at work deserves to be paid more than I do.
24. When people are bossy to me, I often do the opposite of what they ask.
25. I'd feel better if I could find someone who would tell me how to solve my problems.
26. A member of my family or a close friend has had a serious illness this past year.
27. I frequently worry that I will do things that I will later be ashamed of.
28. I become very uncomfortable if I must speak before a large group.
29. I have too many arguments with people when I love them.
30. I don't feel very self-confident these days.
31. I am frequently late for work.
32. People who continually pester me are asking for a punch in the nose.

8

THE MIND TEST

DIRECTIONS: Blacken in the boxes under T (True) or F (False) to show your response to each question. Be careful to see that the number you mark is the same as the number of the question you are answering.

T F	T F	T F	T F	T F	T F	T F	T F
1. ☐ ☐	2. ☐ ☐	3. ☐ ☐	4. ☐ ☐	5. ☐ ☐	6. ☐ ☐	7. ☐ ☐	8. ☐ ☐
9. ☐ ☐	10. ☐ ☐	11. ☐ ☐	12. ☐ ☐	13. ☐ ☐	14. ☐ ☐	15. ☐ ☐	16. ☐ ☐
17. ☐ ☐	18. ☐ ☐	19. ☐ ☐	20. ☐ ☐	21. ☐ ☐	22. ☐ ☐	23. ☐ ☐	24. ☐ ☐
25. ☐ ☐	26. ☐ ☐	27. ☐ ☐	28. ☐ ☐	29. ☐ ☐	30. ☐ ☐	31. ☐ ☐	32. ☐ ☐
33. ☐ ☐	34. ☐ ☐	35. ☐ ☐	36. ☐ ☐	37. ☐ ☐	38. ☐ ☐	39. ☐ ☐	40. ☐ ☐

T F	T F	T F	T F	T F	T F	T F	T F
41. ☐ ☐	42. ☐ ☐	43. ☐ ☐	44. ☐ ☐	45. ☐ ☐	46. ☐ ☐	47. ☐ ☐	48. ☐ ☐
49. ☐ ☐	50. ☐ ☐	51. ☐ ☐	52. ☐ ☐	53. ☐ ☐	54. ☐ ☐	55. ☐ ☐	56. ☐ ☐
57. ☐ ☐	58. ☐ ☐	59. ☐ ☐	60. ☐ ☐	61. ☐ ☐	62. ☐ ☐	63. ☐ ☐	64. ☐ ☐
65. ☐ ☐	66. ☐ ☐	67. ☐ ☐	68. ☐ ☐	69. ☐ ☐	70. ☐ ☐	71. ☐ ☐	72. ☐ ☐
73. ☐ ☐	74. ☐ ☐	75. ☐ ☐	76. ☐ ☐	77. ☐ ☐	78. ☐ ☐	79. ☐ ☐	80. ☐ ☐

T F	T F	T F	T F	T F	T F	T F	T F
81. ☐ ☐	82. ☐ ☐	83. ☐ ☐	84. ☐ ☐	85. ☐ ☐	86. ☐ ☐	87. ☐ ☐	88. ☐ ☐
89. ☐ ☐	90. ☐ ☐	91. ☐ ☐	92. ☐ ☐	93. ☐ ☐	94. ☐ ☐	95. ☐ ☐	96. ☐ ☐
97. ☐ ☐	98. ☐ ☐	99. ☐ ☐	100. ☐ ☐	101. ☐ ☐	102. ☐ ☐	103. ☐ ☐	104. ☐ ☐
105. ☐ ☐	106. ☐ ☐	107. ☐ ☐	108. ☐ ☐	109. ☐ ☐	110. ☐ ☐	111. ☐ ☐	112. ☐ ☐
113. ☐ ☐	114. ☐ ☐	115. ☐ ☐	116. ☐ ☐	117. ☐ ☐	118. ☐ ☐	119. ☐ ☐	120. ☐ ☐

THE MIND TEST

DIRECTIONS: Blacken in the boxes under T (True) or F (False) to show your response to each question. Be careful to see that the number you mark is the same as the number of the question you are answering.

	T	F		T	F		T	F		T	F		T	F		T	F		T	F		T	F
1.	☐	☐	2.	☐	☐	3.	☐	☐	4.	☐	☐	5.	☐	☐	6.	☐	☐	7.	☐	☐	8.	☐	☐
9.	☐	☐	10.	☐	☐	11.	☐	☐	12.	☐	☐	13.	☐	☐	14.	☐	☐	15.	☐	☐	16.	☐	☐
17.	☐	☐	18.	☐	☐	19.	☐	☐	20.	☐	☐	21.	☐	☐	22.	☐	☐	23.	☐	☐	24.	☐	☐
25.	☐	☐	26.	☐	☐	27.	☐	☐	28.	☐	☐	29.	☐	☐	30.	☐	☐	31.	☐	☐	32.	☐	☐
33.	☐	☐	34.	☐	☐	35.	☐	☐	36.	☐	☐	37.	☐	☐	38.	☐	☐	39.	☐	☐	40.	☐	☐

	T	F		T	F		T	F		T	F		T	F		T	F		T	F		T	F
41.	☐	☐	42.	☐	☐	43.	☐	☐	44.	☐	☐	45.	☐	☐	46.	☐	☐	47.	☐	☐	48.	☐	☐
49.	☐	☐	50.	☐	☐	51.	☐	☐	52.	☐	☐	53.	☐	☐	54.	☐	☐	55.	☐	☐	56.	☐	☐
57.	☐	☐	58.	☐	☐	59.	☐	☐	60.	☐	☐	61.	☐	☐	62.	☐	☐	63.	☐	☐	64.	☐	☐
65.	☐	☐	66.	☐	☐	67.	☐	☐	68.	☐	☐	69.	☐	☐	70.	☐	☐	71.	☐	☐	72.	☐	☐
73.	☐	☐	74.	☐	☐	75.	☐	☐	76.	☐	☐	77.	☐	☐	78.	☐	☐	79.	☐	☐	80.	☐	☐

	T	F		T	F		T	F		T	F		T	F		T	F		T	F		T	F
81.	☐	☐	82.	☐	☐	83.	☐	☐	84.	☐	☐	85.	☐	☐	86.	☐	☐	87.	☐	☐	88.	☐	☐
89.	☐	☐	90.	☐	☐	91.	☐	☐	92.	☐	☐	93.	☐	☐	94.	☐	☐	95.	☐	☐	96.	☐	☐
97.	☐	☐	98.	☐	☐	99.	☐	☐	100.	☐	☐	101.	☐	☐	102.	☐	☐	103.	☐	☐	104.	☐	☐
105.	☐	☐	106.	☐	☐	107.	☐	☐	108.	☐	☐	109.	☐	☐	110.	☐	☐	111.	☐	☐	112.	☐	☐
113.	☐	☐	114.	☐	☐	115.	☐	☐	116.	☐	☐	117.	☐	☐	118.	☐	☐	119.	☐	☐	120.	☐	☐

33. I can work easily even if someone is watching me.
34. I become irritated when things don't go well.
35. Lately I've noticed that my hand shakes when I reach for something.
36. I am comfortable reading articles about snakes.
37. When I'm with my family, I feel as if I'm an outsider.
38. I like to flirt.
39. I don't know what to do with my spare time after work.
40. I generally try to cover up my poor opinion of others.
41. I often feel uncomfortable about how different I am from other people.
42. I am currently satisfied with my sex life.
43. I often worry that I may suddenly become angry with someone.
44. I fear that I may die before I accomplish my goals in life.
45. I currently feel that I would not choose the same romantic partner if I had it to do all over again.
46. My appetite is good these days.
47. I hate to go back to work after the weekend.
48. I very seldom disagree with people.
49. I often think it is my destiny to carry out an important mission on earth.
50. Lately I watch television more than ever.
51. I sweat easily even when it's cool.
52. The thought of touching a corpse does not bother me.
53. At the moment my romantic future looks very bright.
54. My daily life is full of interesting things.
55. I hope my child (or child if I had one) will follow in a career similar to mine.
56. Lately when I'm with my friends, I don't feel as if I'm part of the group.
57. I like myself just the way I am.
58. I was in (or came very close to having) an automobile accident in the last six months.
59. Often I'm too excited to sleep at night.
60. I suspect that I have a phobia.
61. My romantic partner and I do not have enough interests in common.
62. I'm not getting along well right now with someone who is important to me.
63. I am as enthusiastic as most people with whom I work.
64. I would like to be seen by others as considerate rather than intelligent.
65. I'm often forced to make excuses for my behavior.
66. It doesn't annoy me to see an adult picking his nose.
67. I seldom have trouble making decisions.
68. The sight of blood upsets me no more than it does anyone else.
69. I am very patient with my child (or with children I know if I have none of my own).
70. I am concerned about my current lack of interest in things.
71. My colleagues at work like me.
72. Lately it is difficult for me to meet new people.
73. I give up on tasks sooner than other people do.
74. I've changed my residence within the last year.
75. I hardly ever worry about what others may think of me.
76. When I go to the dentist, I am not at all nervous.
77. I often get jealous of my spouse's (or family's) outside activities.
78. I would feel better if I didn't take things so seriously.
79. I don't get to use my talents in the job that I have.
80. I can be comfortable with all kinds of people.
81. I am confident that I can do something about the problems that may arise in my life.
82. I get so preoccupied that I forget where I've put things.
83. I'm worried about how I am doing on this test.
84. Whenever I get into an elevator, I think about the cable breaking.
85. I can really depend on my family.
86. All food tastes the same to me lately.
87. I see my job primarily as a way to make enough money so I can enjoy the other things in life.

88. Lately I wish I could trade my friends in for new ones.
89. I sometimes have the feeling that I don't really know myself.
90. During the past year I have had frequent headaches or stomach problems.
91. It disturbs me to think about the shortness of life.
92. When I try something new, I become tense or nervous.
93. Other families seem to get along better than ours.
94. I am hopeful about the future.
95. The job that I have is a real bore.
96. People have taken advantage of my friendship.
97. I have a long way to go before I become the kind of person I want to be.
98. I seldom have a drink or take a pill to try to relax.
99. It hardly bothers me at all when I make a social error.
100. Lately I'm afraid of what might happen to me when I leave the house.
101. Sometimes I think that the members of my family don't really care about one another.
102. Sex doesn't interest me as much as it used to.
103. If I won a lot of money, one of the first things I would do would be to quit my job.
104. I feel uncomfortable going to parties.
105. I'm almost always trying to figure myself out.
106. Someone I was very close to has died within the past year.
107. People often describe me as high-strung.
108. I am not bothered by flying in an airplane.
109. My partner is very sensitive to my sexual needs and desires.
110. I cry easily these days.
111. At the end of a day at work I am eager to leave.
112. Sometimes I wish I could tell people where to get off.
113. I believe that life is more a game of chance than a game of skill.
114. I have taken a new job within the past year.
115. Lately it's been difficult for me to relax.
116. I avoid going to parks or on camping trips because who knows what's out there.
117. My parents tried to control my life too much.
118. I feel downhearted and blue these days.
119. Time seems to fly when I'm at work.
120. Most people seem to understand how I feel about things.

HOW TO SCORE
THE MIND TEST

After you have answered all 120 questions, slip the answer sheet under the front cover, which will serve as a scoring key. In order to line up the answer sheet, be certain that the boxes at the bottom of the page appear totally white.

To find your score, add up the number of blackened boxes that show through the circles in each of the eight vertical columns. Record those sums in the white boxes at the bottom. The box with the highest number indicates the chapter that you should read first. You may then wish to go on to the chapter corresponding to the next highest score, and so forth.

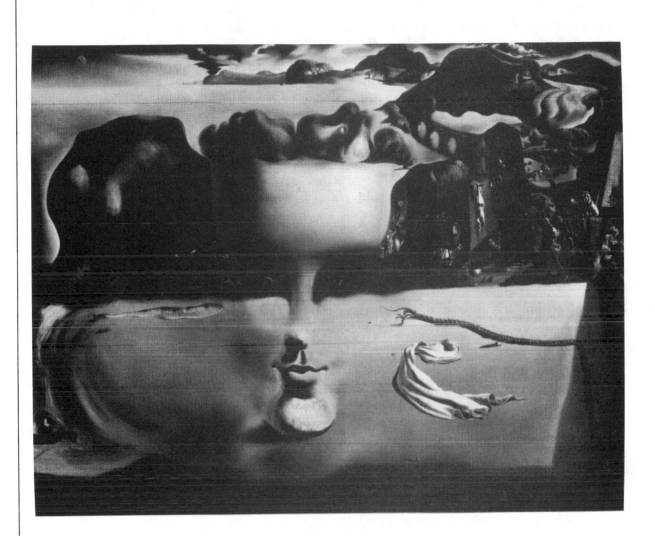

C H A P T E R   O N E

Personality
Analysis

What quality of the mind makes each person absolutely unique, and why is that quality so hard to pin down with a word, a theory, or a test? While the forces of science are converging on all the great physical mysteries—from the origins of the universe to the biochemical secrets of life—the subject of the human personality is as elusive as ever. We do know in practice how to differentiate ourselves from others, and how to tell the others apart; yet the psychological models of personality thus far constructed are as diverse and contradictory as fifteenth-century theories of global navigation. In terms of truly mapping the human personality, the behavioral sciences are still arguing over whether the world is flat or round.

Despite the confusion about human personality at the grandest theoretical level, an accurate and useful science of personality assessment has evolved. It has become possible to measure specific behavioral traits and analyze various components of the individual's personality. Most "personality tests," however, are not at all meant to define the *total* personality, but to measure its various aspects and tendencies. A great deal of thought, experimentation, and very rigorous standards go into the construction of these tests. There are universally accepted standards for weighing the validity, reliability, and significance of each one. There is no test in existence, however, that can be guaranteed to apply to every person individually.

A facet of personality can be selected from a theoretical model, and a test can be constructed to measure something about that trait. For example, Jung's theories about the human psyche included a dimension of introversion-extroversion. Simply defined, this divides the world into those people whose thoughts, words, and actions are directed primarily at the external world, and those people whose behavior is turned inward, toward their private internal world. Psychologists who were interested in testing Jung's theory devised written tests which help in the differentiation of introverts and extroverts. They constructed questions and then tried to predict something about people's behavior from their scores on the test. These tests are known as *theoretical scales*.

But it is not necessary to have a theoretical model to construct a test. The other strategy of test construction involves *empirical scales* because they are evolved through experimentation instead of derived from theory. Questions are assembled and given to two groups of people who are clearly different in some way, then the answers are examined to determine which questions differentiate the groups. If known extroverts answer a question in a particular way, then that question can be used to measure extroversion, along with other similarly tested items.

The assessment of personality is an especially sensitive area when it comes to the diagnosis and treatment of personality disorders. While personality tests can be an invaluable guide to self-knowledge, they should only be used under the direction of a licensed psychotherapist if their purpose is diagnosis or therapy. If you are not suffering from a behavioral or emotional disorder, it is possible to gain self-knowledge and sometimes to effect a positive change in your personality by using tests to point out both your weaknesses and strong points.

Social Desirability Scale

by Douglas P. Crowne
and David Marlowe

Listed below are a number of statements concerning personal attitudes and traits. Read each item and decide whether the statement is true (T) or false (F) as it pertains to you personally. It's best to go with your first judgment and not spend too long mulling over any one question. Place a mark in the space next to each question. Take this test before reading further.

T or F

1. Before voting I thoroughly investigate the qualifications of all the candidates. 1. _____
2. I never hesitate to go out of my way to help someone in trouble. 2. _____
3. It is sometimes hard for me to go on with my work if I am not encouraged. 3. _____
4. I have never intensely disliked anyone. 4. _____
5. On occasions I have had doubts about my ability to succeed in life. 5. _____
6. I sometimes feel resentful when I don't get my way. 6. _____
7. I am always careful about my manner of dress. 7. _____
8. My table manners at home are as good as when I eat out in a restaurant. 8. _____
9. If I could get into a movie without paying and be sure I was not seen I would probably do it. 9. _____
10. On a few occasions, I have given up something because I thought too little of my ability. 10. _____
11. I like to gossip at times. 11. _____
12. There have been times when I felt like rebelling against people in authority even though I knew they were right. 12. _____
13. No matter who I'm talking to, I'm always a good listener. 13. _____
14. I can remember "playing sick" to get out of something. 14. _____
15. There have been occasions when I have taken advantage of someone. 15. _____
16. I'm always willing to admit it when I make a mistake. 16. _____
17. I always try to practice what I preach. 17. _____
18. I don't find it particularly difficult to get along with loudmouthed, obnoxious people. 18. _____
19. I sometimes try to get even rather than forgive and forget. 19. _____
20. When I don't know something I don't mind at all admitting it. 20. _____
21. I am always courteous, even to people who are disagreeable. 21. _____
22. At times I have really insisted on having things my own way. 22. _____
23. There have been occasions when I felt like smashing things. 23. _____
24. I would never think of letting someone else be punished for my wrong-doings. 24. _____
25. I never resent being asked to return a favor. 25. _____
26. I have never been irked when people expressed ideas very different from my own. 26. _____
27. I never make a long trip without checking the safety of my car. 27. _____
28. There have been times when I was quite jealous of the good fortune of others. 28. _____
29. I have almost never felt the urge to tell someone off. 29. _____
30. I am sometimes irritated by people who ask favors of me. 30. _____
31. I have never felt that I was punished without cause. 31. _____
32. I sometimes think when people have a misfortune they only got what they deserved. 32. _____
33. I have never deliberately said something that hurt someone's feelings. 33. _____

SCORING THE SCALE

To find your score, fold this page forward on the dotted line and compare your answers to those listed on the Scoring Key. Count the number of times the answers you marked *agree* with the ones listed on the Scoring Key and write that number in the box below. Your total score can range from a low of zero agreement to a high of 33.

TOTAL SCORE

FOLD FORWARD TO SCORE

SCORING KEY

1. T _____
2. T _____
3. F _____
4. T _____
5. F _____
6. F _____
7. T _____
8. T _____
9. F _____
10. F _____
11. F _____
12. F _____

13. T _____
14. F _____
15. F _____
16. T _____
17. T _____
18. T _____
19. F _____
20. T _____
21. T _____
22. F _____
23. F _____
24. T _____
25. T _____
26. T _____
27. T _____
28. F _____
29. T _____
30. F _____
31. T _____
32. F _____
33. T _____

INTERPRETING YOUR SCORE

Low Scorers (0–8)—If you scored in this range, you (a) answered most of the questions in a socially *undesirable* direction, but (b) answered them in a way more honest and true to real life than most people. There are a couple of interesting reasons why you may have answered in this way. One may be that you are very comfortable with who you are; you do not feel discomfort when other people view you as behaving in a socially undesirable way. A second explanation may be that you want to be seen by others as a social rebel, someone who is different. Perhaps, too, it's your way of holding a part of your personality out to others and daring them to reject it. If the first mentioned reason is also true, that you are comfortable with how and who you are, then a low level of social desirability may not cause you any trouble. If, however, answering in a rebellious manner does reflect some difficulties you have in getting along with others, then some of the suggestions listed for high scorers may also be useful for you.

Average Scorers (9–19)—If you scored in this range, you are scoring as two out of three people do when taking the test. Scores here represent a combination of socially desirable and socially undesirable responses. Hopefully, this combination represents a balance for you in your day-to-day behavior. It may be helpful for you to look back over the questions and think about how your responses actually relate to your true behavior in those situations.

High Scorers (20–33)—Your score in this range suggests that being seen as socially acceptable is very important to you. (Of course, you have to consider where you scored within this range to decide how much these statements are true for you.) Perhaps your score indicates what Drs. Crowne and Marlowe see as a need for approval from others. If so, a high level of this need for approval can adversely affect your social interactions; you may be seeking approval while presenting a distorted picture of what you're really like. If a high need for approval describes you, you may feel frequent social insecurity, or anxiety about doing what others expect. If it's causing you discomfort, some professional counseling may help you. Counseling can provide you with an arena for evaluating your feelings about self-worth, adequacy, and acceptability. If you are a very high scorer, you're aware of how much energy it takes to constantly fulfill the "ideal" of social expectations. You will probably feel a lot better in the long run if you can redirect some of that energy into continued self-examination and understanding.

ABOUT THE SCALE

In the 1950s, psychologists began noticing that the desire to be seen as socially acceptable was also a major factor in how people answered psychological tests. Regardless of what the question was about, people tended to select the answer that was more flattering, more socially acceptable, over answers that were less desirable, less "nice." To investigate what had by then become labeled "social desirability," psychologists Douglas Crowne and David Marlowe assembled a group of questions that represented behaviors that are, at the same time, culturally sanctioned as "right" but very unlikely to occur in reality.

An example of this type of item is, "I never hesitate to go out of my way to help someone in trouble." The "true" response is socially desirable; the "false" response is socially undesirable. Probably most people would like to be seen as "never hesitating to help," but it would be a rare individual indeed who *always* went out of his or her way to help someone in trouble. In keeping with other criteria used by Crowne and Marlowe in selecting their questions, it is important to note that neither the socially acceptable nor the socially unacceptable response has any implication of mental or emotional instability. The answer a person chooses actually measures how he likes to view himself and be seen by others in terms of socially desirable attitudes and behaviors.

By now you can probably see why we suggested that you take the test before reading further. Imagine what it would be like trying to answer the questions "honestly" after reading this discussion of what the test attempts to measure. You might, in fact, find it interesting to go back over the questions, and see what changes in any of your answers would do to your level of social desirability.

Locus of Control Scale

by Stephen Nowicki, Jr.,
and B. Strickland

Here are the directions Drs. Nowicki and Strickland include with their scale:

We are trying to find out what men and women think about certain things. We want you to answer the following questions the way you feel. There are no right or wrong answers. Don't take too much time answering any one question, but do try to answer them all.

One of your concerns during the test may be, "What should I do if I can answer both yes and no to a question?" It's not unusual for that to happen. If it does, think about whether your answer is just a little more one way than the other. For example, if you'd assign a weighting of 51 percent to "yes" and assign 49 percent to "no," mark the answer "yes." Try to pick one or the other response for all questions and not leave any blank.

Mark your responses to the question on the answer sheet in the next column. When you are finished, turn the page to score your test.

YES	NO
1. _____	1. _____
2. _____	2. _____
3. _____	3. _____
4. _____	4. _____
5. _____	5. _____
6. _____	6. _____
7. _____	7. _____
8. _____	8. _____
9. _____	9. _____
10. _____	10. _____
11. _____	11. _____
12. _____	12. _____
13. _____	13. _____
14. _____	14. _____
15. _____	15. _____
16. _____	16. _____
17. _____	17. _____
18. _____	18. _____
19. _____	19. _____
20. _____	20. _____
21. _____	21. _____
22. _____	22. _____
23. _____	23. _____
24. _____	24. _____
25. _____	25. _____
26. _____	26. _____
27. _____	27. _____
28. _____	28. _____
29. _____	29. _____
30. _____	30. _____
31. _____	31. _____
32. _____	32. _____
33. _____	33. _____
34. _____	34. _____
35. _____	35. _____
36. _____	36. _____
37. _____	37. _____
38. _____	38. _____
39. _____	39. _____
40. _____	40. _____

1. Do you believe that most problems will solve themselves if you just don't fool with them?
2. Do you believe that you can stop yourself from catching a cold?
3. Are some people just born lucky?
4. Most of the time do you feel that getting good grades meant a great deal to you?
5. Are you often blamed for things that just aren't your fault?
6. Do you believe that if somebody studies hard enough he or she can pass any subject?
7. Do you feel that most of the time it doesn't pay to try hard because things never turn out right anyway?
8. Do you feel that if things start out well in the morning it's going to be a good day no matter what you do?
9. Do you feel that most of the time parents listen to what their children have to say?
10. Do you believe that wishing can make good things happen?
11. When you get punished does it usually seem it's for no good reason at all?
12. Most of the time do you find it hard to change a friend's opinion?
13. Do you think that cheering more than luck helps a team to win?
14. Did you feel that it was nearly impossible to change your parents' minds about anything?
15. Do you believe that parents should allow children to make most of their own decisions?
16. Do you feel that when you do something wrong there's very little you can do to make it right?
17. Do you believe that most people are just born good at sports?
18. Are most of the other people your age stronger than you are?
19. Do you feel that one of the best ways to handle most problems is just not to think about them?
20. Do you feel that you have a lot of choice in deciding who your friends are?
21. If you find a four-leaf clover, do you believe that it might bring you good luck?
22. Did you often feel that whether or not you did your homework had much to do with what kind of grades you got?
23. Do you feel that when a person your age is angry at you, there's little you can do to stop him or her?
24. Have you ever had a good-luck charm?
25. Do you believe that whether or not people like you depends on how you act?
26. Did your parents usually help you if you asked them to?
27. Have you felt that when people were angry with you it was usually for no reason at all?
28. Most of the time, do you feel that you can change what might happen tomorrow by what you do today?
29. Do you believe that when bad things are going to happen they just are going to happen no matter what you try to do to stop them?
30. Do you think that people can get their own way if they just keep trying?
31. Most of the time do you find it useless to try to get your own way at home?
32. Do you feel that when good things happen they happen because of hard work?
33. Do you feel that when somebody your age wants to be your enemy there's little you can do to change matters?
34. Do you feel that it's easy to get friends to do what you want them to do?
35. Do you usually feel that you have little to say about what you get to eat at home?
36. Do you feel that when someone doesn't like you there's little you can do about it?
37. Did you usually feel that it was almost useless to try in school because most other children were just plain smarter than you were?
38. Are you the kind of person who believes that planning ahead makes things turn out better?
39. Most of the time, do you feel that you have little to say about what your family decides to do?
40. Do you think it's better to be smart than to be lucky?

SCORING THE SCALE

Using the Scoring Key below, fold this page back on the dotted line and compare your answers on the previous page to the ones on the key. Give yourself one point each time your answer agrees with the keyed answer. Your score is the total number of agreements between your answers and the ones on the key.

SCORING KEY

1. Yes _____
2. No _____
3. Yes _____
4. No _____
5. Yes _____
6. No _____
7. Yes _____
8. Yes _____
9. No _____
10. Yes _____
11. Yes _____
12. Yes _____
13. No _____
14. Yes _____
15. No _____
16. Yes _____
17. Yes _____
18. Yes _____
19. Yes _____
20. No _____
21. Yes _____
22. No _____
23. Yes _____
24. Yes _____
25. No _____
26. No _____
27. Yes _____
28. No _____
29. Yes _____
30. No _____
31. Yes _____
32. No _____
33. Yes _____
34. No _____
35. Yes _____
36. Yes _____
37. Yes _____
38. No _____
39. Yes _____
40. No _____

TOTAL SCORE

FOLD BACK TO SCORE

INTERPRETING YOUR SCORE

Low Scorers (0–8)—Scores from zero to eight represent the range for about one third of the people taking the test. As a low scorer, you probably see life as a game of skill rather than chance. You most likely believe that you have a lot of control over what happens to you, both good and bad. With that view, internal locus of control people tend to take the initiative in everything from job-related activities to relationships and sex. You are probably described by others as vigilant in getting things done, aware of what's going on around you, and willing to spend energy in working for specific goals. You would probably find it quite frustrating to sit back and let others take care of you, since you stressed on the test that you like to have your life in your own hands.

Although taking control of your life is seen as the "best way to be," psychologists caution that it has its own set of difficulties. Someone who is responsible for his or her own successes is also responsible for failures. So if you scored high in this direction, be prepared for the downs as well as the ups.

Average Scorers (9–16)—Since you've answered some of the questions in each direction, internal and external control beliefs for you may be situation specific. You may look at one situation, work, for example, and believe that your rewards are externally determined, that no matter what you do you can't get ahead. In another situation, love perhaps, you may see your fate as resting entirely in your own hands. You will find it helpful to review the questions and group them into those you answered in the internal direction and those you answered in the external direction. Any similarities in the kinds of situations within one of the groups? If so, some time spent thinking about what it is in those situations that makes you feel as though the control is or is not in your hands can help you better understand yourself.

High Scorers (17–40)—Scores in this range represent the external control end of the scale. Only about 15 percent of the people taking the test score 17 or higher. As a high scorer, you're saying that you see life generally more as a game of chance than as one where your skills make a difference.

There are, however, many different reasons for any individual to score in the external control direction. For example, psychologists have found that people in many minority and disadvantaged groups tend to score in the external direction. One recent suggestion for such scores is that people in these groups perceive their life situations realistically. In general, blacks, women, and lower-socioeconomic-class individuals really do have more restrictions on their own successes— fewer job options, lower pay, less opportunity for advancement—in many cases no matter what they do or don't do. An *internal* locus of control belief in such situations would be quite unrealistic and inappropriate. Thus your own high external control score could be a realistic perception of your current life circumstances.

On the other hand, your score may represent a strong belief in luck or superstition and a concurrent feeling of helplessness in controlling your life. Research studies have shown a relationship between unrealistic external control beliefs and problems like anxiety, depression, low self-concept, and poor physical health. Only you can decide exactly how much of your external belief system is accurate and how much of it is inappropriate given your life situation. If any of the emotional and/or physical problems listed do fit your view of your own life, professional help is definitely called for and very likely to produce positive results. But you'll have to take the initiative and make the first major move to regain control—or the belief of control—over your own life.

ABOUT THE SCALE

Do you believe in luck? Is it something like luck or chance or the actions of others that determines what happens to you? Or do you see the direction of your life determined by your own actions? These two views represent the extremes of a personality concept labeled "locus of control." This concept is concerned with whether an individual believes in an internal or an external control of his life.

In 1954, psychologist Julian Rotter was supervising Dr. E. Jerry Phares as he conducted therapy with a single, twenty-three-year-old man in a Veterans Administration Mental Hygiene Clinic. As therapy moved along, Drs. Rotter and Phares noted that Karl's (not his real name) problems were not of the common variety—at least not common to the Freudian understanding used in therapy before and during the 1950's. In recalling the therapy, Dr. Phares writes, "It gradually dawned on the clinician that Karl did not perceive any causal relationship between his behavior and the occurrence of rewards. He attributed such occurrences to luck or other factors over which he had no control. Once the clinician realized this, Karl's behavior made sense."

Over the next twelve years, Drs. Phares and Rotter jointly and separately pursued the concept labeled "locus of control." Dr. Rotter culminated this work in 1966 by publishing the first Locus of Control Scale. That test attempted to measure how we perceive the relationship between our own actions and the consequences of those actions. Dr. Rotter felt that we learn from past life experiences whether to believe that our rewards and punishments depend on our own actions or on those of people around us.

After hundreds of research studies investigating Rotter's test and the locus of control concept, psychologists Stephen Nowicki, Jr., and B. Strickland developed a related but significantly different test. With the publishing of their scale, Drs. Nowicki and Strickland attempted to deal with certain criticisms that had been leveled at Rotter's test, and, in addition, make it possible to measure locus of control in children. In 1974, Dr. Nowicki and a colleague, Dr. Marshall Duke, revised the earlier Nowicki-Strickland scale into the adult test we have included here.

Self-Acceptance Scale

by Emanuel M. Berger

On the next page are a series of statements that ask about personal feelings. Read each one carefully and decide how true or false that statement is for you. Using the scale provided below, mark your answer on the answer sheet in the next column.

1 = Completely true
2 = Mostly true
3 = Half true, half false
4 = Mostly false
5 = Completely false

1. _____
2. _____
3. _____
4. _____
5. _____
6. _____
7. _____
8. _____
9. _____
10. _____
11. _____
12. _____
13. _____
14. _____
15. _____
16. _____
17. _____
18. _____
19. _____
20. _____
21. _____
22. _____
23. _____
24. _____
25. _____
26. _____
27. _____
28. _____
29. _____
30. _____
31. _____
32. _____
33. _____
34. _____
35. _____
36. _____

1. I'd like it if I could find someone who would tell me how to solve my personal problems.

2. I don't question my worth as a person, even if I think others do.

3. When people say nice things about me, I find it difficult to believe they really mean it. I think maybe they're kidding me or just aren't being sincere.

4. If there is any criticism or anyone says anything about me, I just can't take it.

5. I don't say much at social affairs because I'm afraid that people will criticize me or laugh if I say the wrong thing.

6. I realize that I'm not living very effectively, but I just don't believe I've got it in me to use my energies in better ways.

7. I look on most of the feelings and impulses I have toward people as being quite natural and acceptable.

8. Something inside me just won't let me be satisfied with any job I've done—if it turns out well, I get a very smug feeling that this is beneath me, I shouldn't be satisfied with this, this isn't a fair test.

9. I feel different from other people. I'd like to have the feeling of security that comes from knowing I'm not too different from others.

10. I'm afraid for people that I like to find out what I'm really like, for fear they'd be disappointed in me.

11. I am frequently bothered by feelings of inferiority.

12. Because of other people, I haven't been able to achieve as much as I should have.

13. I am quite shy and self-conscious in social situations.

14. In order to get along and be liked, I tend to be what people expect me to be rather than anything else.

15. I seem to have a real inner strength in handling things. I'm on a pretty solid foundation and it makes me pretty sure of myself.

16. I feel self-conscious when I'm with people who have a superior position to mine in business or at school.

17. I think I'm neurotic or something.

18. Very often, I don't try to be friendly with people because I think they won't like me.

19. I feel that I'm a person of worth, on an equal plane with others.

20. I can't avoid feeling guilty about the way I feel toward certain people in my life.

21. I'm not afraid of meeting new people. I feel that I'm a worthwhile person and there's no reason why they should dislike me.

22. I sort of only half believe in myself.

23. I'm very sensitive. People say things and I have a tendency to think they're criticizing me or insulting me in some way and later when I think of it, they may not have meant anything like that at all.

24. I think I have certain abilities and other people say so too. I wonder if I'm not giving them an importance way beyond what they deserve.

25. I feel confident that I can do something about the problems that may arise in the future.

26. I guess I put on a show to impress people. I know I'm not the person I pretend to be.

27. I do not worry or condemn myself if other people pass judgment against me.

28. I don't feel very normal, but I want to feel normal.

29. When I'm in a group, I usually don't say much for fear of saying the wrong thing.

30. I have a tendency to sidestep my problems.

31. Even when people do think well of me, I feel sort of guilty because I know I must be fooling them—that if I were really to be myself, they wouldn't think well of me.

32. I feel that I'm on the same level as other people and that helps to establish good relations with them.

33. I feel that people are apt to react differently to me than they would normally react to other people.

34. I live too much by other people's standards.

35. When I have to address a group, I get self-conscious and have difficulty saying things well.

36. If I didn't always have such hard luck, I'd accomplish much more than I have.

SCORING KEY

	A	B
1.	_____	
2. Reverse		_____
3.	_____	
4.	_____	
5.	_____	
6.	_____	
7. Reverse		_____
8.	_____	
9.	_____	
10.	_____	
11.	_____	
12.	_____	
13.	_____	
14.	_____	
15. Reverse		_____
16.	_____	
17.	_____	
18.	_____	
19. Reverse		_____
20.	_____	
21. Reverse		_____
22.	_____	
23.	_____	
24.	_____	
25. Reverse		_____
26.	_____	
27. Reverse		_____
28.	_____	
29.	_____	
30.	_____	
31.	_____	
32. Reverse		_____
33.	_____	
34.	_____	
35.	_____	
36.	_____	

TOTAL SCORE

FOLD BACK TO SCORE

SCORING THE SCALE

To score the scale, fold this page back along the dotted line to line up your answers with the Scoring Key.

First, transfer your answers into the spaces in column A for items 1, 3, 4, 5, etc.

Next, in column B, reverse the numerical value of your answers for items 2, 7, 15, 19, etc. For example:

In column B, an answer of

1 earns 5 points

2 earns 4 points

3 earns 3 points

4 earns 2 points

5 earns 1 point

To find your final score, add together the totals of columns A and B and record them in the box marked "total score."

INTERPRETING YOUR SCORE

Low Scorers (0–110)—Low scorers on this scale are expressing little self-acceptance. Such a score can be interpreted as reflecting a negative view of the self and a feeling that others have a negative view as well. If you scored here, look at where you scored within this range. Scores near 110 may not be cause for concern. Scores significantly lower than that, however, should be regarded with much concern. Low self-acceptance influences much of what you do, from your confidence level at work and your sensitivity with friends to feelings of worth at home. Several programs, such as assertiveness training and personal growth groups, specifically direct their efforts to such problems. In addition, individual professional help can be useful in providing you with an avenue for objective self-examination. It will be difficult for you to share life with others until you can feel more accepting of yourself.

Average Scorers (111–150)—It is not easy to interpret a normal or average level of self acceptance because such acceptance varies with your roles in life. This means that you may confront a situation one day in which you bubble with confidence, and yet feel that you could have done much better in a different situation the next day. This level of self-accept-ance describes the way most of us are, praising ourselves one moment, condemning ourselves the next. For most of us, this is an accurate reflection of our skills and our striving to do better. The important part of such a view is that we have accurate perceptions of when we are doing well and when we could have done better. Goals that are set unreasonably high (for whatever reasons) reduce the positive feelings that our behavior may really deserve. The line between average and high self-acceptance may not be in our skill level but rather in our attitude about what we must do before we will pat ourselves on the back.

High Scorers (151–180)—If you are a high scorer, your level of self-acceptance is such that this scale can't tell you anything new. You are stating on this scale that you consider yourself a confident and worthy individual. Others probably find you easy to talk to, since you report that you accept both praise and criticism from others in an objective fashion. In addition, you are likely to base your behavior on internalized values and accept the responsibility for whatever the consequences of your behavior may be. You feel comfortable about your ability to handle any problems or challenges that arise and overall have good feelings toward life.

ABOUT THE SCALE

The picture each of us has about him or herself is a portrait based largely on information provided to us by our social experiences. We are almost constantly adding information from our environment about the effects of our attitudes and behavior on others and their reactions to us. Such social reactions form the basis for our feelings about other people and help us develop our view of what each of us is like as a person. For many years psychologists have been interested in the role of the self-image in personality development. How much and how well we accept what we see as our "self" is an important part of our emotional health.

One of the earliest scales to measure the self-image and the acceptance of self was developed by psychologist Emanuel Berger. His first, and perhaps most formidable, task was that of defining "self-acceptance." Relying on previous work by Dr. Elizabeth Scheerer and Dr. Carl Rogers, Dr. Berger listed nine characteristics of the self-accepting person, such as "Has faith in his capacity to cope with life." This formulation led to the development and selection of a final group of thirty-six items for his Self-Acceptance Scale. This scale is in frequent use today in psychological research and clinical work regarding self-esteem and self-acceptance.

Change Seeker Index

by Warren K. Garlington and Helen E. Shimota

Beginning below are 95 statements that deal with your personal preferences and with how you view yourself. If the statement describes the way you see yourself, mark true (T) for that item. If the statement does not describe you, mark false (F). Your first response is probably best. To record your answers, tear out the answer sheet on the next page. A duplicate of the answer sheet is printed on the back.

1. I think a strong will power is a more valuable gift than a well-informed imagination.
2. I like to read newspaper accounts of murders and other forms of violence.
3. I like to conform to custom and to avoid doing things that people I respect might consider unconventional.
4. I would like to see a bullfight in Spain.
5. I would prefer to spend vacations in this country, where you know you can get a good holiday, than in foreign lands that are colorful and "different."
6. I often take pleasure in certain nonconforming attitudes and behaviors.
7. In general, I would prefer a job with a modest salary, but guaranteed security rather than one with large but uncertain earnings.
8. I like to feel free to do what I want to do.
9. I like to follow instructions and to do what is expected of me.
10. Because I become bored easily, I need plenty of excitement, stimulation, and fun.
11. I like to complete a single job or task at a time before taking on others.
12. I like to be independent of others in deciding what I want to do.
13. I am well described as a meditative person, given to finding my own solutions instead of acting on conventional rules.
14. I much prefer symmetry to asymmetry.
15. I often do whatever makes me feel cheerful here and now, even at the cost of some distant goal.
16. I can be friendly with people who do things which I consider wrong.
17. I tend to act impulsively.
18. I like to do routine work using a good piece of machinery or apparatus.
19. People view me as a quite unpredictable person.
20. I think society should be quicker to adopt new customs and throw aside old habits and mere traditions.
21. I prefer to spend most of my leisure hours with my family.
22. In traveling abroad, I would rather go on an organized tour than plan for myself the places I will visit.
23. I like to have lots of lively people around me.
24. I like to move about the country and to live in different places.
25. I feel that what this world needs is more steady and "solid" citizens rather than "idealists" with plans for a better world.
26. I like to dabble in a number of different hobbies and interests.
27. I like to avoid situations where I am expected to do things in a conventional way.
28. I like to have my life arranged so that it runs smoothly and without much change in my plans.
29. I like to continue doing the same old things rather than to try new and different things.
30. I would like to hunt lions in Africa.
31. I find myself bored by most tasks after a short time.
32. I believe that it is not a good idea to think too much.
33. I always follow the rule: business before pleasure.
34. I enjoy gambling for small stakes.
35. Nearly always I have a craving for more excitement.
36. I enjoy doing "daring," foolhardy things "just for fun."
37. I see myself as an efficient, businesslike person.

ANSWER SHEET

(Tear Out)

1. _____	20. _____	39. _____	58. _____	77. _____
2. _____	21. _____	40. _____	59. _____	78. _____
3. _____	22. _____	41. _____	60. _____	79. _____
4. _____	23. _____	42. _____	61. _____	80. _____
5. _____	24. _____	43. _____	62. _____	81. _____
6. _____	25. _____	44. _____	63. _____	82. _____
7. _____	26. _____	45. _____	64. _____	83. _____
8. _____	27. _____	46. _____	65. _____	84. _____
9. _____	28. _____	47. _____	66. _____	85. _____
10. _____	29. _____	48. _____	67. _____	86. _____
11. _____	30. _____	49. _____	68. _____	87. _____
12. _____	31. _____	50. _____	69. _____	88. _____
13. _____	32. _____	51. _____	70. _____	89. _____
14. _____	33. _____	52. _____	71. _____	90. _____
15. _____	34. _____	53. _____	72. _____	91. _____
16. _____	35. _____	54. _____	73. _____	92. _____
17. _____	36. _____	55. _____	74. _____	93. _____
18. _____	37. _____	56. _____	75. _____	94. _____
19. _____	38. _____	57. _____	76. _____	95. _____

ANSWER SHEET

(Tear Out)

1. _____	20. _____	39. _____	58. _____	77. _____
2. _____	21. _____	40. _____	59. _____	78. _____
3. _____	22. _____	41. _____	60. _____	79. _____
4. _____	23. _____	42. _____	61. _____	80. _____
5. _____	24. _____	43. _____	62. _____	81. _____
6. _____	25. _____	44. _____	63. _____	82. _____
7. _____	26. _____	45. _____	64. _____	83. _____
8. _____	27. _____	46. _____	65. _____	84. _____
9. _____	28. _____	47. _____	66. _____	85. _____
10. _____	29. _____	48. _____	67. _____	86. _____
11. _____	30. _____	49. _____	68. _____	87. _____
12. _____	31. _____	50. _____	69. _____	88. _____
13. _____	32. _____	51. _____	70. _____	89. _____
14. _____	33. _____	52. _____	71. _____	90. _____
15. _____	34. _____	53. _____	72. _____	91. _____
16. _____	35. _____	54. _____	73. _____	92. _____
17. _____	36. _____	55. _____	74. _____	93. _____
18. _____	37. _____	56. _____	75. _____	94. _____
19. _____	38. _____	57. _____	76. _____	95. _____

38. I like to wear clothing that will attract attention.
39. I cannot keep my mind on one thing for any length of time.
40. I enjoy arguing even if the issue isn't very important.
41. It bothers me if people think I am being too unconventional or odd.
42. I see myself as a practical person.
43. I never take medicine on my own, without a doctor's ordering it.
44. From time to time I like to get completely away from work and anything that reminds me of it.
45. At times I have been very anxious to get away from my family.
46. My parents have often disapproved of my friends.
47. There are several areas in which I am prone to do things quite unexpectedly.
48. I would prefer to be a steady and dependable worker than a brilliant but unstable one.
49. In going places, eating, working, etc., I seem to go in a very deliberate, methodical fashion rather than rush from one thing to another.
50. It annoys me to have to wait for someone.
51. I get mad easily and then get over it soon.
52. I find it hard to keep my mind on a task or job unless it is terribly interesting.
53. For me planning one's activities well in advance is very likely to take most of the fun out of life.
54. I like to go to parties and other affairs where there is lots of loud fun.
55. I enjoy lots of social activity.
56. I enjoy thinking up unusual or different ideas to explain everyday events.
57. I seek out fun and enjoyment.
58. I like to experience novelty and change in my daily routine.
59. I like a job that offers change, variety, and travel, even if it involves some danger.
60. In my job I appreciate constant change in the type of work to be done.
61. I have the wanderlust and am never happy unless I am roaming or traveling about.
62. I have periods of such great restlessness that I cannot sit long in a chair.
63. I like to travel and see the country.
64. I like to plan out my activities in advance, and then follow the plan.
65. I like to be the center of attention in a group.
66. When I get bored I like to stir up some excitement.
67. I experience periods of boredom with respect to my job.
68. I admire a person who has a strong sense of duty to the things he believes in more than a person who is brilliantly intelligent and creative.
69. I like a job that is steady enough for me to become expert at it rather than one that constantly challenges me.
70. I like to finish any job or task that I begin.
71. I feel better when I give in and avoid a fight than I would if I tried to have my own way.
72. I don't like things to be uncertain and unpredictable.
73. I am known as a hard and steady worker.
74. I would like the job of foreign correspondent for a newspaper.
75. I used to feel sometimes that I would like to leave home.
76. I find my interests change quite rapidly.
77. I am continually seeking new ideas and experiences.
78. I like continually changing activities.
79. I get a lot of bright ideas about all sorts of things—too many to put into practice.
80. I like being amid a great deal of excitement and bustle.
81. I feel a person just can't be too careful.
82. I try to avoid any work which involves patient persistence.
83. Quite often I get "all steamed up" about a project, then lose interest in it.
84. I would rather drive 5 miles under the speed limit than 5 miles over it.
85. Most people bore me.
86. I like to find myself in new situations where I can explore all the possibilities.
87. I much prefer familiar people and places.
88. When things get boring, I like to find new and unfamiliar experiences.
89. If I don't like something, I let people know about it.
90. I prefer a routine way of life to an unpredictable one full of change.
91. I feel that people should avoid behavior or situations that will call undue attention to themselves.
92. I am quite content with my life as I am now living it.
93. I would like to be absent from work (school) more often than I actually am.
94. Sometimes I want to leave home, just to explore the world.
95. My life is full of change because I make it so.

SCORING KEY

1. F	20. T	39. T	58. T	77. T
2. T	21. F	40. T	59. T	78. T
3. F	22. F	41. F	60. T	79. T
4. T	23. T	42. F	61. T	80. T
5. F	24. T	43. F	62. T	81. F
6. T	25. F	44. T	63. T	82. T
7. F	26. T	45. T	64. F	83. T
8. T	27. T	46. T	65. T	84. F
9. F	28. F	47. T	66. T	85. T
10. T	29. F	48. F	67. T	86. T
11. F	30. T	49. F	68. F	87. F
12. T	31. T	50. T	69. F	88. T
13. T	32. F	51. T	70. F	89. T
14. F	33. F	52. T	71. F	90. F
15. T	34. T	53. T	72. F	91. F
16. T	35. T	54. T	73. F	92. F
17. T	36. T	55. T	74. T	93. T
18. F	37. F	56. T	75. T	94. T
19. T	38. T	57. T	76. T	95. T

SCORING THE INDEX

To find your score, compare the answer sheet with the Scoring Key on the facing page. Give yourself one point each time your answer agrees with the answer on the key. Write the total number of agreements in the box below.

**TOTAL
SCORE**

INTERPRETING YOUR SCORE

Low Scorers (0–35)—People who score in this range are showing a low desire for change. Of course, the intensity of their desire (or lack of desire) for change depends on where in this range they scored. Such scores can indicate either a comfort with the way things are or an uneasiness with the possibility of new experiences. If you are a low scorer, you are probably described by others as calm and easygoing, though at the extreme, these behaviors could appear as inhibited and "uptight." Only you can decide whether to interpret your low change seeker score as a positive or negative description of the way you see your life at present. If you do feel inhibited and not as spontaneous as you would like, some small changes may be worth a try. Go slowly with these changes, however, since an increase in stimulation brings associated stress which you may not be ready for.

Average Scorers (36–55)—Average scorers are reporting a normal, typical level of change seeking. This is probably seen in your day-to-day life as instances of contentment with the way things are combined with occasional feelings of wanderlust and a desire for something new and different. There are probably a few areas in which you prefer spiciness over a bland existence. If, for example, you have a routine type of job, your avocations probably fulfill your need for thrill seeking and disinhibition. The reverse is also a possibility, where you may work in a job with almost constant change and then desire a quiet, predictable life at home.

High Scorers (56–95)—High scorers are reporting a high desire for change. Again, the intensity of that desire relates directly to where within this range your score falls. Descriptions of high scorers often include outgoing, high energy, thrill seeking, disinhibited, and other terms which relate to a desire for new experiences. If you are a high scorer, you probably find yourself uncomfortable in a job and related situations that involve primarily clerical or routine tasks. You may also find that your desire for change bothers others, since they see you as too impulsive or as always out to change the way things are. In many cases, high scorers find that they need to work on controlling their desire for change in order to make maximum effective use of their creative and original ideas.

ABOUT THE INDEX

We need things to change. Our perception and interpretation of the world around us rely on the objects in our environment changing in some way. In cases where the objects do not move, we move; we walk around, we bob our heads up and down, all to see things in a different light. And where neither we nor the object can move, our perceptual system takes over, producing fascinating movement in optical illusions. This type of need for change is at a basic level, and it is true for all of us.

But people differ markedly when it comes to the need for more complex changes. This need can be seen in someone acting impulsively, having varied hobbies, or traveling extensively. These are the types of changes that psychologists Warren Garlington and Helen Shimota used as the basis for their Change Seeker Index. They first defined "change seeking" as "an habitual, consistent pattern of behavior which acts to control the amount and kind of stimulus input a given organism receives." Thus if someone always preferred abstract art over paintings of still life, a roller coaster over a merry-go-round, and hot, spicy foods over potatoes, we could assume this person had a need for stimulation and change. Drs. Garlington and Shimota then developed 211 items, some from other personality tests and some which they created, to measure a need for change. After initial research, they narrowed the index to the 95 statements we have included here.

Their work with the Change Seeker Index has combined with that of other researchers investigating the effects of boredom and monotony on behavior and attitudes. The need for such concern was forcefully presented by Alvin Toffler in his popular book *Future Shock*. As one psychologist wrote, "Toffler views our technology as rushing headlong into ever-increasing rates of change and novelty, creating an information flow so rapid that human beings can no longer adapt to it." It has become important, given the nature of our lives, to understand both individual and collective needs, and the need for change is among the most important.

Self-Image Checklist

by Elliot A. Weiner

Read the adjectives listed below. Place an X in the column labeled "As I Actually Am" for each word that describes you as you see yourself now. Then, disregarding the marks you just made, go back and read through the list again. This time place an O in the column labeled "As I Would Like to Be" for each word that describes the way you would like to be if you could be your ideal person.

	(X) AS I ACTUALLY AM	(O) AS I WOULD LIKE TO BE
emotional		
opinionated		
humorous		
independent		
friendly		
ambitious		
interesting		
honest		
attractive		
reserved		
enthusiastic		
average		
sensitive		
dependable		
intelligent		
lazy		
cheerful		
envious		
energetic		
considerate		
quiet		
clever		
bossy		
resilient		
self-centered		
fragile		
sincere		
relaxed		
forceful		
cynical		
impulsive		
apathetic		

SCORING THE CHECKLIST

To find your score, give yourself one point for each time the columns you've filled out match. A match is a word followed by *both* an X and an O—or by *neither* an X nor an O. If only one column is marked, it is *not* a match. Add up your total score and place it in the box below.

TOTAL SCORE

INTERPRETING YOUR SCORE

It is important for you to establish your own cutoff levels of high and low scores for a list such as this one. There are no studies which say that most people agree on a certain number of the words. The concepts involved in examining your self-image through this process are almost in opposition to any firm score cutoffs. We do offer the idea that agreement on 75 percent of the adjectives (a score of 24 or above) suggests a reasonable level of comfort with who you are. But it would not be unreasonable for you to match on all but one or two words and have those characteristics be very important ones. In fact they could be so meaningful to you that not being as you would like on those traits could produce high levels of frustration. It may also be just as possible that you have learned to accept not being as you would like; thus a bothersome discrepancy for someone else would not be a conflict for you. Reflecting on what these traits mean and how important possessing them is to you will add depth to your self-knowledge and provide a truer picture of your self-image regardless of your actual score.

ABOUT THE CHECKLIST

We, as humans, are in the unique position of being able to stand outside ourselves and to describe, judge, and critique the way we are. The self is the most important thing in the world to us. What we do, how we feel, and who we are center around how we see that part of us that we consider the self.

Both philosophers and psychologists have recognized the need to study the individual and his self-image. Plato instructed us, "Know thyself"; Alfred Adler contended that a "tendency to disparage others" arose out of feelings of inferiority; and Erich Fromm urged us to "love ourselves, for self-love and the love of others go hand in hand." At first glance, studying such a topic would seem difficult, since it is a personal and private concern. The psychologist primarily responsible for developing research techniques for self-image and for integrating the concept into therapy was Dr. Carl Rogers. Dr. Rogers noted that many of his clients in therapy had a negative self-image, a lack of congruence between what they wanted to be like and how they saw themselves at that time. Such discrepancies between how we see ourselves and how we would like to be form an *actual-self* and *ideal-self* conflict, and can give rise to frustration, stress, and low self-esteem. For some of us the conflict can appear overwhelming and can lead to depression; for others such conflict can serve to energize us toward the goals we have in life.

To aid in providing you with that information about your actual-self and ideal-self views, we have presented a list of thirty-two adjectives, representing a cross section of positive and negative characteristics. Use of a list such as this one stems directly from the work and ideas of Dr. Rogers. The list is truly a nontest; there are no rights or wrongs, only information about how you see yourself.

Fear of Appearing Incompetent Scale

by Lawrence R. Good
and Katherine C. Good

The thirty-six statements on the next page refer to feelings that all of us share to varying degrees. Read each one and decide if the statement is true (T) or false (F) as it pertains to you personally. Though some may be difficult to answer, do answer each one. Record your answers on the answer sheet in the next column.

T or F

1. _____
2. _____
3. _____
4. _____
5. _____
6. _____
7. _____
8. _____
9. _____
10. _____
11. _____
12. _____
13. _____
14. _____
15. _____
16. _____
17. _____
18. _____
19. _____
20. _____
21. _____
22. _____
23. _____
24. _____
25. _____
26. _____
27. _____
28. _____
29. _____
30. _____
31. _____
32. _____
33. _____
34. _____
35. _____
36. _____

1. I would never worry about the possibility of being judged a fool in some activities.
2. I would very much like to be less apprehensive about my capabilities.
3. I would not be prone to worry about my supervisory abilities if I were in a supervisory position.
4. I tend to be concerned about not being effective enough in my dealings with others.
5. After having had a conversation with someone, I have a tendency to worry about having said something that was inappropriate.
6. I am not prone to be apprehensive or worried about my ability to do a task well.
7. I am prone to worry sometimes that others may think I am not intelligent enough for my job.
8. I am frequently prone to take actions to counteract previous bad impressions which I believe I have made.
9. I would never be at all apprehensive or worried about my adequacy in handling business transactions.
10. After completing an assignment or task, I am prone to have doubts about whether I did it right.
11. I am never concerned about the possibility that others may regard me as being somewhat odd or strange.
12. I rarely worry about being considered by others to be misinformed or ignorant about certain things.
13. I am occasionally concerned about the possibility of being considered to have inappropriate friendships.
14. I have a tendency to worry that others will consider my behavior in some activities to be inappropriate or tactless.
15. I am almost never concerned about the possibility of being regarded as spastic or clumsy around others.
16. I have a tendency to worry that others may regard me as not knowing what is really going on in the immediate social situation.
17. I tend to worry about the possibility of displaying inappropriate etiquette at a formal social event.
18. I would never worry about my adequacy in sexual relationships.
19. I would never worry about the possibility of failing to meet the work standards at my place of employment.
20. I might be inclined to avoid criticizing someone else's judgment for fear of appearing to be in the wrong.
21. I tend to worry that others will think I am not keeping up with my work.
22. I am rarely concerned about my adequacy in physical or athletic events.
23. If I were functioning in a professional field, I would not worry about my relationships with fellow professionals.
24. I am prone to worry that others may regard my beliefs and opinions as incorrect or funny.
25. I tend to worry that others may think that I am not keeping well enough informed about the developments in my field.
26. I am prone to worry about my adequacy in classroom work or activities.
27. I would never worry about the possibility of saying something inappropriate in a new social situation.
28. I tend to worry that others may think I don't know what I'm doing.
29. I have a tendency to worry that others will laugh at my ideas.
30. I am rarely concerned about whether others will take me seriously enough.
31. I am prone to worry that my parents or friends will regard me as irresponsible or undependable.
32. If I were functioning as a salesperson, I would not worry about the possibility of appearing to be clumsy in my handling of clients or customers.
33. I tend to fear that others may see me as not sufficiently self-disciplined.
34. I tend to worry that others may think I am not devoting enough energy or enthusiasm to my work.
35. I would never worry about the possibility that others might feel I have poor judgment in some situations.
36. I would never worry about appearing to be in over my head or beyond my capabilities in my line of work or my course of study.

SCORING KEY

TOTAL SCORE

1. F _____
2. T _____
3. F _____
4. T _____
5. T _____
6. F _____
7. T _____
8. T _____
9. F _____
10. T _____
11. F _____
12. F _____
13. T _____
14. T _____
15. F _____
16. T _____
17. T _____
18. F _____
19. F _____
20. T _____
21. T _____
22. F _____
23. F _____
24. T _____
25. T _____
26. T _____
27. F _____
28. T _____
29. T _____
30. F _____
31. T _____
32. F _____
33. T _____
34. T _____
35. F _____
36. F _____

FOLD BACK TO SCORE

SCORING THE SCALE

To find your score, fold this page back along the dotted line and compare your answers on the previous page to those on the Scoring Key. Give yourself one point for each match. Your total score equals the total number of agreements.

INTERPRETING YOUR SCORE

Low Scorers (0–12)—Low scorers are reporting little worry about feeling incompetent in their interpersonal behavior. If you are a low scorer, you are likely seen by others as confident in your work and social activities. You are stating on this scale that you have a low need to maintain face and do not go into activities worried that you will look foolish. Such personal feelings suggest that you also know your own strengths and are accepting of your deficiencies. The psychological term that is often used to describe such a self-directed individual is "self-actualized," suggesting someone with a high level of self-acceptance and self-esteem.

Average Scorers (13–22)—If you scored in this range, you are in the company of most people. Scores here suggest a normal combination of self-confidence and apprehension involving your perception of how you will perform in various situations. Your life is likely to be a mix of times when you feel as confident as a superhero and other times when you feel more like Bozo the Clown. Most people have gotten used to this combination of feelings and regard them as "just the way they are." Some, however, are not willing to accept the uncomfortable times, yet cannot specify their concerns enough to work on reducing them. If this last statement describes you, a combination of self-examination and the information from some of the other tests in this book will help.

High Scorers (23–36)—Most high scorers spend considerable energy worrying about appearing incompetent regardless of the situation. Although such fears may be strongest in one particular type of activity, your score here suggests a general lack of self-acceptance and a fear that others will find you unacceptable as well. Scores near the bottom of this range may be those of a typically average scorer involved in a stress situation which has temporarily increased self-doubt. In that case, the interpretation for average scorers may be more accurate for you. Higher scores, however, suggest the need for serious self-examination. A fear of appearing incompetent can make it difficult for you to act spontaneously, since spontaneity increases your chance for making mistakes. Such fear also can inhibit close personal relationships, job success, and personal growth. Further tests can assist you in pinpointing specific problem areas and, if combined with professional help, increase your self-understanding and enjoyment of life.

ABOUT THE SCALE

Psychologists who study our lifelong developmental processes divide our lifetimes into certain stages. Some, such as Swiss psychologist Jean Piaget, have studied intellectual development and the way our abilities to think, reason, and solve problems change as we get older. Associated with our cognitive maturation, however, are stages involving the social- and self-concept aspects of our personality. These *psychosocial* stages are those in which we establish new orientations to ourselves and to other people in our social world. According to Dr. Erik Erikson, a psychoanalyst, we progress through eight stages from infancy to old age, with each having the potential for a particular conflict related to the way we see ourselves and our social environment. The earliest stages involve development of trust (vs. mistrust), autonomy (vs. self-doubt), initiative (vs. guilt), and industry (vs. inferiority). According to Dr. Erikson, how we handle these preadolescent stages largely determines the view we will have of ourselves during later life, for they lead to "a sense of knowing where one is going, and an inner assuredness of anticipated recognition from those who count."

The quality of such assuredness relates to how comfortable we are with our abilities and to the degree we worry about looking incompetent. If we know our own strengths and are accepting of our limitations, we will, most likely, not be faced with frequent worry about making mistakes or looking foolish. If, on the other hand, this assuredness is lacking in us, worry about our abilities, judgment, and overall adequacy could be a constant companion.

Although theoretical positions about this area of self-regard were plentiful in the early 1970s, two psychologists, Drs. Lawrence and Katherine Good, saw the need for a measure of personal views of competency. Their rationale behind the items which they selected for the scale was:

. . . either situations in which an individual might reasonably worry about his competency, as perceived by others, or of his attributes on which he might worry about possible negative evaluation from others—being perceived by others, for example, as not intelligent enough for one's job.

The resulting thirty-six items formed the Fear of Appearing Incompetent Scale which we have included here.

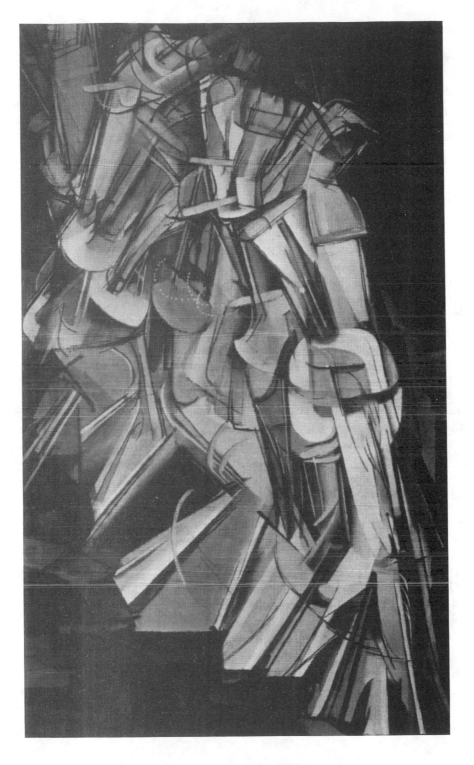

CHAPTER TWO

Stress

*S*tress may be a recent concept to medical circles and to the general public, but it is a very old phenomenon—as old as life itself. As soon as the first single-celled creature appeared on earth, stress became an integral part of life. In fact, stress is the price we all pay for the struggle to stay alive.

The most widely accepted definition of stress is that of Dr. Hans Selye, the man who worked patiently and painstakingly for over fifty years to establish the scientific basis for a study of stress. According to Dr. Selye, "Stress is the non-specific response of the body to any demand made upon it." When your health or survival is threatened by the environment, your body reacts in both a specific and a nonspecific way. Meeting the immediate threat to survival is the specific response; the biological surge of alarm you feel is the nonspecific response.

In a sense, stress is an artifact of our long, violent, prehistoric evolution. When a threat appears on the horizon—in the old days it might have been a mastodon, but today it is more likely to be a mugger—our fight-or-flight reaction releases hormones that prepare the body for battle. This powerful nonspecific response puts potentially dangerous stress on the heart, the circulation, and the endocrine system. Yet in this current environment we call civilization, we no longer have to resolve physical conflicts daily, and the stressful components of our fight-flight reactions are becoming more evident. Those hormones that get us all charged up can also cause internal wear and tear—metabolic by-products of those reactions can clog your arteries. Too much adrenaline can raise the blood pressure dangerously. Stress can act as a trigger for heart disease, circulatory ailments, pulmonary problems, cancer, and mental and emotional illness.

Stress is all around us. Anything that makes you adjust, adapt, or change is stress. You don't have to be in a dangerous environment to experience high levels of stress in your life. If you are sitting in your office, talking to your girl friend on the phone, and the boss walks in and catches you, that is stress. If your boss calls you into his office and gives you an unexpected promotion and raise, that too is stress. Stress is the slight cold you've been running while you work, and stress is also the noise outside your window. If someone close to you has died, if you owe or inherit a large sum of money, you are being subjected to stress. Dr. Selye points out, "Normal activities—a game of tennis or even a passionate kiss—can produce considerable stress."

In order to deal with the stress in your life, you must know where that stress originates and how you habitually react to it. The tests in this section are designed to measure those two broad factors: the sources of the stress in your particular environment, and your unique pattern of coping with those stresses.

Life Change Index Scale

by Thomas Holmes

Look over the events listed in the Life Change Index Scale. Place a check (√) in the space next to a given event if it has happened to you within the last twelve months. Turn the page to find your score.

#	Event		Score
1.	Death of spouse	1. _____	100
2.	Divorce	2. _____	73
3.	Marital separation from mate	3. _____	65
4.	Detention in jail or other institution	4. _____	63
5.	Death of a close family member	5. _____	63
6.	Major personal injury or illness	6. _____	53
7.	Marriage	7. _____	50
8.	Being fired at work	8. _____	47
9.	Marital reconciliation	9. _____	45
10.	Retirement from work	10. _____	45
11.	Major change in the health or behavior of a family member	11. _____	44
12.	Pregnancy	12. _____	40
13.	Sexual difficulties	13. _____	39
14.	Gaining a new family member (e.g., through birth, adoption, oldster moving in, etc.)	14. _____	39
15.	Major business readjustment (e.g., merger, reorganization, bankruptcy, etc.)	15. _____	38
16.	Major change in financial state (e.g., either a lot worse off or a lot better off than usual)	16. _____	37
17.	Death of a close friend	17. _____	36
18.	Changing to a different line of work	18. _____	36
19.	Major change in the number of arguments with spouse (e.g., either a lot more or a lot less than usual regarding child-rearing, personal habits, etc.)	19. _____	35
20.	Taking on a mortgage greater than $10,000 (e.g., purchasing a home, business, etc.)	20. _____	31
21.	Foreclosure on a mortgage or loan	21. _____	30
22.	Major change in responsibilities at work (e.g., promotion, demotion, lateral transfer)	22. _____	29
23.	Son or daughter leaving home (e.g., marriage, attending college, etc.)	23. _____	29
24.	In-law troubles	24. _____	29
25.	Outstanding personal achievement	25. _____	28
26.	Spouse beginning or ceasing work outside the home	26. _____	26
27.	Beginning or ceasing formal schooling	27. _____	26
28.	Major change in living conditions (e.g., building a new home, remodeling, deterioration of home or neighborhood)	28. _____	25
29.	Revision of personal habits (dress, manners, associations, etc.)	29. _____	24
30.	Troubles with the boss	30. _____	23
31.	Major change in working hours or conditions	31. _____	20
32.	Change in residence	32. _____	20
33.	Changing to a new school	33. _____	20
34.	Major change in usual type and/or amount of recreation	34. _____	19
35.	Major change in church activities (e.g., a lot more or a lot less than usual)	35. _____	19
36.	Major change in social activities (e.g., clubs, dancing, movies, visiting, etc.)	36. _____	18
37.	Taking on a mortgage or loan less than $10,000 (e.g., purchasing a car, TV, freezer, etc.)	37. _____	17
38.	Major change in sleeping habits (a lot more or a lot less sleep or change in time of day when asleep)	38. _____	16
39.	Major change in number of family get-togethers (e.g., a lot more or a lot less than usual)	39. _____	15
40.	Major change in eating habits (a lot more or a lot less food intake, or very different meal hours or surroundings)	40. _____	15
41.	Vacation	41. _____	13
42.	Christmas	42. _____	12
43.	Minor violations of the law (e.g., traffic tickets, jaywalking, disturbing the peace, etc.)	43. _____	11

Reprinted with permission from the *Journal of Psychosomatic Research*, II, 213–218, "The Holmes and Rahe Social Readjustment Rating Scale," copyright © 1967, Pergamon Press, Inc., New York.

SCORING THE SCALE

Add up the number of points next to each of your check marks. Place the total in the box below.

TOTAL LIFE CHANGE UNITS (LCU)

INTERPRETING YOUR SCORE

Dr. Holmes and his colleagues have clearly shown the relationship between recent life changes and future illness. Listed below are the score categories and the associated probability of illness during the next two years for a person with that score.

0–150	No significant problem
150–199	Mild Life Crisis level with a 35 percent chance of illness
200–299	Moderate Life Crisis Level with a 50 percent chance of illness
300 or over	Major Life Crisis Level with an 80 percent chance of illness

It is not only your life change unit (LCU) total score that is related to your likelihood of illness. Also important with your amount of change is how you respond to those changes. Psychologists have found that when they match two groups, both with LCU totals over 300, those who developed physical illnesses had more difficulty in coping emotionally with life changes than those who did not get sick. Aspects of how you go through your daily life, such as feeling the need to get everything done right on time, also are involved in how you handle potentially troublesome levels of life changes.

This means that after you total your LCUs, you also need to think about how emotionally strong you are to handle those changes and how good your present techniques are for relaxing and easing the pressure.

Your own LCU may suggest a higher—or lower—probability of illness depending on how you deal with stress as it arises. Just being aware of the concept of stress and how life changes increase stress can reduce your own likelihood of getting ill. You can reduce the stress of adjusting to change even further by developing specific techniques, such as relaxation, hobbies, exercise, and meditation.

ABOUT THE SCALE

The most common stress-producing situations in modern life involve fear and frustration. Most people would agree that there is a high degree of stress involved in negative events related to these two emotions, events such as death of a spouse, marital separation, or going to jail. But it took a group of researchers at the University of Washington School of Medicine to point out and quantify that *any* major life change, even a positive one, produces stress. The research team, led by Dr. Thomas Holmes, found in a group of 400 people a high relationship between their amount of life changes during the previous six months and their likelihood of getting sick.

Out of such research came the Life Change Index Scale which rates 43 life events on the degree of stress each produces. The subsequent research needed to validate the scale is fascinating. The study mentioned earlier involved having 400 people count their *life change units* (LCU) over a six-month and one-year period with the researcher then predicting, on the basis of LCU totals, which people would develop a major health problem during the next six months. Another study measured LCU totals in a group of 2684 Navy and Marine personnel getting ready for a six-month cruise and predicted which people would need the most visits to sick bay during the cruise. Yet another research project involved the prediction of football injuries during a season on the basis of LCU totals for team members before the season began. In each of these studies, plus numerous others, life change unit totals were highly related to the likelihood of any specific person developing a major health problem.

As you look over the events, you will notice that an event such as marital separation produces more stress than a personal illness or injury. But the positive change of getting back together, marital reconciliation, produces more stress than a situation involving sex difficulties. Dr. Holmes and his colleagues were among the first researchers to quantify what stress expert Dr. Hans Selye had said for several years, that we must watch out for the impact of positive life changes as well as those that are clearly negative. As Drs. Holmes and Masuda wrote, "If it takes too much effort to cope with the environment, we have less to spare for preventing disease. When life is too hectic and when coping attempts fail, illness is the unhappy result."

The Annoyance List

Below is a list containing types of people and various daily occurrences. If the situation or person described is annoying to you, place a check next to the statement.

_____ 1. A person telling me how to drive.
_____ 2. A person acting in an affected manner.
_____ 3. Getting a telephone busy signal.
_____ 4. To see reckless driving.
_____ 5. To hear a loud talker.
_____ 6. To see an adult picking his nose.
_____ 7. A person telling me to do something when I am just about to do it.
_____ 8. A person continually criticizing something.
_____ 9. A person being sarcastic.
_____ 10. To wait for someone to come to the phone.
_____ 11. To know a person is staring at me.
_____ 12. To have my thoughts interrupted.
_____ 13. A person putting his hands on me unnecessarily.
_____ 14. A person adjusting my TV set.
_____ 15. A person giving me a weak handshake.
_____ 16. A person picking his teeth.
_____ 17. A person who "can't leave the party."
_____ 18. A person continually trying to be funny.
_____ 19. Being asked almost constantly to do something.
_____ 20. To be evaluated critically by a relative stranger.
_____ 21. To hear a person use "shock words."
_____ 22. To have to walk on slippery sidewalks.
_____ 23. To listen to politicians make promises.
_____ 24. To hear a person talking during a musical number.
_____ 25. To hear "loud" music.
_____ 26. To be unable to find a bus seat.
_____ 27. A person watching me work.
_____ 28. To hear a person swear.
_____ 29. To see overaffectionate demonstration between members of the same sex.
_____ 30. To hear disparaging remarks about a member of a minority group.
_____ 31. A man frequently referring to his girlfriends.
_____ 32. A woman frequently referring to her boyfriends.
_____ 33. Too much discussion of sex on a date.
_____ 34. To have to kiss an unattractive relative.
_____ 35. To see public lovemaking.
_____ 36. A person talking a great deal and not saying anything very important.
_____ 37. To listen to a sales pitch.
_____ 38. To have "too many" TV commercials.
_____ 39. A person interrupting me when I am talking.
_____ 40. To see a person spit.
_____ 41. To have a hostess repeatedly urging me to take some food I do not want.
_____ 42. Not being able to find the rattle in the car.
_____ 43. To discover that the library book is not there.
_____ 44. To see colors that clash.
_____ 45. To see an untidy room.
_____ 46. To find a hair in my food.
_____ 47. To have a hole in my stocking or sock.
_____ 48. The classmate who talks too much.
_____ 49. Not to be listened to.
_____ 50. To be given impractical suggestions.

Adapted from Instructor's Manual to accompany *Psychology*, B. von Haller Gilmer, Harper & Row, 1973.

SCORING AND INTERPRETATION

There are no score ranges or specific cutoff points for this list; it is just that—a list of types of people and situations. Some research has suggested that most people find approximately 15 to 20 of these items annoying, but its main use is that of providing you with information about how you, personally, feel about these daily situations.

As you look back over the list, think about how those annoyances that you've checked add to your daily stress level. If you've checked only a few, you are probably seen as an easygoing person, someone not under (or at least not showing) a lot of minor daily stresses. If, however, you have checked a lot of these annoyances, you may find yourself "uptight" much of the time each day—at least more stressed than you would like. The information is here for you to use in furthering your self-understanding and in deciding whether or not you need to change your level of frustration and stress.

**TOTAL
SCORE**

ABOUT THE LIST

Many psychological tests say, "There are no right or wrong answers," yet when you answer the questions, it feels to you as though there are. For the Annoyance List, there really is no right or wrong check mark. We have included the list here in the chapter on stress because of the relationship between frustration, irritability, and stress.

You have no doubt encountered many of the people and situations described in the Annoyance List. When one of them does annoy you, you can usually *feel* your annoyance: your heart starts beating faster, your teeth clench, your stomach tightens. You are feeling the stress of frustration. And it follows that the greater the number of day-to-day events that annoy you, the higher your level of stress.

You might want to let your spouse or other friends check their annoyances as well. It may be fun—and meaningful—to compare the annoyances you've each checked. For example, many people find that number 8, "A person continually criticizing something," is annoying. Few, on the other hand, check number 44, "To see colors that clash," as annoying. After the two of you have gone through the list, discuss what it is about that type of person or that situation that makes it annoying to one or both of you. Since a large part of a psychological test is self-understanding, such discussion could provide useful information about you and your feelings about others.

Physical Anxiety Questionnaire

by Lawrence R. Good
and Chester C. Parker

Read each of the twenty-four statements below. For each one, decide whether the statement is true (T) or false (F) for you personally. Mark your answer in the appropriate space next to each statement. If you are unsure about an answer, decide if the statement is slightly more true than false (T) or slightly more false than true (F).

_____ 1. I sometimes worry about not being in good physical condition.

_____ 2. I sometimes worry about eating too many unhealthy foods.

_____ 3. I sometimes worry about the appearance or condition of my teeth.

_____ 4. I sometimes worry about the appearance or condition of my hair.

_____ 5. I sometimes worry about not getting enough exercise.

_____ 6. I sometimes worry about pains in my back or side.

_____ 7. I sometimes worry about the condition of my skin.

_____ 8. I sometimes worry about having bad breath.

_____ 9. I sometimes worry about having unpleasant body odor.

_____ 10. I sometimes worry about the appearance of my nose, mouth, or cheeks.

_____ 11. I sometimes worry about the appearance of my hands or fingernails.

_____ 12. I sometimes worry about the appearance of my legs or feet.

_____ 13. I sometimes worry about having a poor speaking voice.

_____ 14. I sometimes worry about putting too much strain on my body.

_____ 15. I sometimes worry about not getting enough sleep.

_____ 16. I sometimes worry about the condition of my lungs.

_____ 17. I sometimes worry about straining my eyes too much.

_____ 18. I sometimes worry about pains in my chest or abdomen.

_____ 19. I sometimes worry about not being able to endure pain very well.

_____ 20. I sometimes worry about not having enough physical strength or stamina for certain activities.

_____ 21. I sometimes worry about getting injured in an accident.

_____ 22. I sometimes worry about the possible harmful effects of certain physical activities I engage in.

_____ 23. I sometimes worry about the physical discomfort or pain of dying.

_____ 24. I sometimes worry about what will happen to my body after death.

SCORING THE QUESTIONNAIRE

Count the number of times that you answered "true" and place that number in the box below. Your score for this questionnaire can range from 0 to 24 statements marked "true."

TOTAL SCORE

INTERPRETING YOUR SCORE

Low Scorers (0–7)—By scoring in this range, you are acknowledging a lower than average number of physical worries. Even if you do have certain physical problems, your score suggests that you do not spend much time worrying about them or other bodily concerns. If this is an accurate picture of how you regard your physical condition, that's great. In times of stress, you are likely to have the necessary emotional energy for handling that stress effectively.

Average Scorers (8–12)—This is the range of scores for the middle one third of the people taking the questionnaire. Your score here says that you do have several areas of bodily concern. This concern, these worries, may stem from one specific major physical problem or many nagging smaller ones. If the latter statement is true for you, you may be leaving yourself open to increased physical problems when you're under high stress. Some of the suggestions for high scorers may be of help to you.

High Scorers (13–24)—Your score here says that you are quite concerned about your physical condition and may be showing several bothersome physical symptoms. Such a high level of worry could make it rough for you in times of stress; your body is likely to reflect that stress with increased physical problems. If that happens, your ability to deal effectively with the cause of the stress could be significantly reduced. Now is a good time for you to deal with those worries and with the physical symptoms themselves. If you've been putting off a medical checkup for fear of having your worries confirmed, schedule the checkup. In the long run, your worries may be more painful than the truth from a physical exam. If you find that your worries are unfounded and yet they persist, counseling can be effective in helping you become more resistant, emotionally and physically, to stress.

ABOUT THE QUESTIONNAIRE

Many of the effects of stress on us as individuals are seen in physical symptoms such as fatigue, bodily aches and pains, and insomnia. However, psychologists have also shown that *worry* about such physical problems is also related to our ability to deal with stressful situations. In using energy for such worry and anxiety, we reduce our system's capabilities to ward off the negative impact of stress. When we encounter the stress the very ailments we worried about invariably become reality.

Psychologists Lawrence Good and Chester Parker designed the Physical Anxiety Questionnaire to measure how much we are worrying about physical problems. Notice that the questionnaire contains statements about worries, not about actual physical problems. Our worries can be more stressful than our actual physical pains.

Stress Quiz

Answer each of the questions below by placing a check in the appropriate column for "yes" or "no." Answer the questions in terms of your own personal experiences and feelings during the past twelve months. To find your score, turn the page.

	NO	YES
1. Have you lived or worked in a noisy area?	___	___
2. Have you changed your living conditions or moved?	___	___
3. Have you had trouble with in-laws?	___	___
4. Have you taken out a large loan or mortgage?	___	___
5. Have you tended to fall behind with the things you should do?	___	___
6. Have you found it difficult to concentrate at times?	___	___
7. Have you frequently had trouble going to sleep?	___	___
8. Have you found that you tend to eat, drink or smoke more than you really should?	___	___
9. Have you watched 3 or more hours of television daily for weeks at a time?	___	___
10. Have you or your spouse changed jobs or work responsibilities?	___	___
11. Have you been dissatisfied or unhappy with your work or felt excessive work responsibility?	___	___
12. Has a close friend died?	___	___
13. Have you been dissatisfied with your sex life?	___	___
14. Have you been pregnant?	___	___
15. Have you had an addition to the family?	___	___
16. Have you worried about making ends meet?	___	___
17. Has one of the family had bad health?	___	___
18. Have you taken tranquilizers from time to time?	___	___
19. Have you frequently found yourself becoming easily irritated when things don't go well?	___	___
20. Have you often experienced bungled human relations—even with those you love most?	___	___
21. Have you found that you're often impatient or edgy with your children or other family members?	___	___
22. Have you tended to feel restless or nervous a lot of the time?	___	___
23. Have you had frequent headaches or digestive upsets?	___	___
24. Have you experienced anxiety or worry for days at a time?	___	___
25. Have you often been so preoccupied that you have forgotten where you've put things (such as keys) or forgotten whether you've turned off appliances on leaving home or office?	___	___
26. Have you been married or reconciled with your spouse?	___	___
27. Have you had a serious accident, illness or surgery?	___	___
28. Has anyone in your immediate family died? Have you divorced or separated?	___	___

SCORING KEY

To score the quiz, fold this page forward on the dotted line. Transfer only your "yes" answers to the scoring key. For each "yes" answer write the number of points you receive next to the appropriate item number.

Add up the points listed for all of the questions to which you answered "yes." Place that number in the box labeled "Total Score for 'Yes' Answers." Your score can range from 0 to 117 points.

FOLD FORWARD TO SCORE

52

SCORING KEY

```
┌─────────┐
│         │
│         │
│         │
└─────────┘
```

TOTAL SCORE
FOR "YES" ANSWERS

1. _____ 3 points
2. _____ 3 points
3. _____ 3 points
4. _____ 3 points
5. _____ 3 points
6. _____ 3 points
7. _____ 3 points
8. _____ 3 points

9. _____ 3 points

10. _____ 4 points
11. _____ 4 points

12. _____ 4 points
13. _____ 4 points
14. _____ 4 points
15. _____ 4 points
16. _____ 4 points
17. _____ 4 points
18. _____ 4 points
19. _____ 4 points

20. _____ 4 points

21. _____ 4 points

22. _____ 4 points
23. _____ 5 points
24. _____ 5 points
25. _____ 5 points

26. _____ 5 points
27. _____ 5 points
28. _____ 6 points
29. _____ 7 points

INTERPRETING YOUR SCORE

Low Scorers (0–15)—This range of scores represents a low level of the kinds of stresses listed in the Stress Quiz. If you scored very low, you're most likely in great shape. If you scored near the upper end of this range, you're reporting some stresses but are probably handling them well. If you do not feel that you are handling the stress in your life as well as you would like to, some of the suggestions listed for the other score levels may be of help to you.

Medium Scorers (16–40)—If you scored in this range, you are reporting between mild and moderate levels of stress. Becoming aware of how much stress you are currently under and what is causing that stress can be very important for you. Part of such helpful self-understanding is a review of what you do on a daily basis to relieve stress as you feel it building up. Some additions or changes in those methods may be called for. Also keep watch on any future events which may add to your level of stress. You may want to delay, avoid, or reschedule some of them.

High Scorers (41–117)—People who score in this high range are reporting great amounts of stress. If you scored here, you are no doubt already aware of the stress level in your life. What you may not be aware of is what exactly is causing that high stress level. You may find it useful to look back over the quiz and notice which specific feelings and events accounted for your high point total. Regardless of what is causing your current stress level, however, it is important for you to do two things. First, avoid, if at all possible, any additional stress until you feel more in control of your life. Second, seek out professional help—your physician or psychologist—for ways to reduce your already high level of stress and for assistance in preventing a continuation of a stress-producing life-style.

ABOUT THE QUIZ

As you saw in taking the Life Change Index Scale, various aspects of our daily lives can be evaluated in terms of how much stress they are likely to produce. Worries and concerns also add to our stress levels and reduce the energy we have for effectively handling stress situations. As part of a program to treat high levels of stress, Audio Health Services developed this Stress Quiz. The quiz is intended primarily to serve as a broad screening instrument, allowing you to estimate your own level of stress.

CHAPTER THREE

Anxiety

*A*lthough it is not a pleasant emotion, anxiety can serve a useful, even vital purpose by preparing you for danger. Anxiety, however, can easily become overpowering, painful, or paralyzing. Estimates suggest that ten million Americans suffer from maladaptive "free-floating" anxiety. Nearly one third of all patients who seek out medical care have unspecifiable anxieties as their primary problem. Severe anxiety is another case of a defense system running amok and turning into an internal enemy when there are no more external enemies to fight.

For instance, imagine walking down a dark street very late at night. You might tend to walk quickly, breathe a little more rapidly, feel your heart race slightly. Your emotions help prepare your body for the possibility of danger. That is an example of a mild, perfectly adaptive form of fear. Now, if you start thinking about being mugged before you even go out on the street because of recent incidences in that neighborhood, your reaction could become more extreme. Your palms might feel sweaty, you might be shaking even though it isn't cold, goosebumps might break out on your arms. When a cat steps out of the shadows, you nearly jump out of your skin. That situation is an example of a normal adaptive fear that has gone over the edge into anxiety.

Even in the more extreme example, your anxiety is still aimed toward a specific purpose directly related to your survival. But suppose that it is midday instead of midnight, that it is your own neighborhood, and the people on the street are your friends and neighbors. If your heart is pounding when you leave the house, your stomach tense, your teeth clenched, and you constantly look behind you in *this* situation, severe anxiety has taken over. There is no longer any adaptive purpose behind your fear.

The explanation of the way that maladaptive anxiety develops is a source of long-standing controversy between behavioral and psychoanalytic psychologists. In the psychoanalytic model, most of us spend a great deal of emotional energy keeping unpleasant or unacceptable urges, fears, and thoughts from becoming conscious. Anxiety develops on the surface when the repressed material, all the unconscious conflicts, threatens to break through our internal barriers and emerge into awareness. In the psychoanalytic system, free-floating anxiety is a symptom of deeper conflicts in the personality.

In the behavioral model, anxiety has a different explanation. Like any other behavior, anxiety is viewed as a learned response to certain stimuli. Your present anxiety when confronted by a dark street was originally caused long ago when you had an unpleasant experience walking home or because you learned of the danger from others. The elements of the situation have become conditioned stimuli that trigger physiological tensions, which you in turn feel as anxiety. In this case, anxiety is a habit, acquired just as you acquire any other habit.

While there is not yet a general agreement about the correct cures or the true causes of anxiety, it is possible to detect and differentiate the kinds and intensities of anxieties through tests. Like stress, anxiety is a fact of modern life, not to be avoided, but to be understood and managed. Locating the source, object, and degree of your own anxieties is the first step toward controlling them.

Fear of Negative Evaluation Scale

by David Watson
and Ronald Friend

Carefully read each of the 30 statements listed below. Decide whether each statement is true (T) or false (F) as it pertains to you personally. If you are unsure which is the better answer, decide which one is slightly more applicable to how you are feeling at the moment and answer accordingly. Try to answer based on your first reaction to the statement. Don't spend too long on any one item.

T or F

1. I rarely worry about seeming foolish to others.
2. I worry about what people will think of me even when I know it doesn't make any difference.
3. I become tense and jittery if I know someone is sizing me up.
4. I am unconcerned even if I know people are forming an unfavorable impression of me.
5. I feel very upset when I commit some social error.
6. The opinions that important people have of me cause me little concern.
7. I am often afraid that I may look ridiculous or make a fool of myself.
8. I react very little when other people disapprove of me.
9. I am frequently afraid of other people noticing my shortcomings.
10. The disapproval of others would have little effect on me.
11. If someone is evaluating me I tend to expect the worst.
12. I rarely worry about what kind of impression I am making on someone.
13. I am afraid that others will not approve of me.
14. I am afraid that people will find fault with me.
15. Other people's opinions of me do not bother me.
16. I am not necessarily upset if I do not please someone.
17. When I am talking to someone, I worry about what they may be thinking about me.
18. I feel that you can't help making social errors sometimes, so why worry about it.
19. I am usually worried about what kind of impression I make.
20. I worry a lot about what my superiors think of me.
21. If I know someone is judging me, it has little effect on me.
22. I worry that others will think I am not worthwhile.
23. I worry very little about what others may think of me.
24. Sometimes I think I am too concerned with what other people think of me.
25. I often worry that I will say or do the wrong things.
26. I am often indifferent to the opinions others have of me.
27. I am usually confident that others will have a favorable impression of me.
28. I often worry that people who are important to me won't think very much of me.
29. I brood about the opinions my friends have about me.
30. I become tense and jittery if I know I am being judged by my superiors.

1. _____
2. _____
3. _____
4. _____
5. _____
6. _____
7. _____
8. _____
9. _____
10. _____
11. _____
12. _____
13. _____
14. _____
15. _____
16. _____
17. _____
18. _____
19. _____
20. _____
21. _____
22. _____
23. _____
24. _____
25. _____
26. _____
27. _____
28. _____
29. _____
30. _____

SCORING THE SCALE

To find your score, fold this page forward on the dotted line and compare your answers to those on the Scoring Key.

Your score for this scale is determined by the number of times that your answers match the ones listed in the Scoring Key. Give yourself one point for each such match and place your total in the box below.

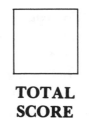

TOTAL SCORE

SCORING KEY

1. F _____
2. T _____
3. T _____
4. F _____
5. T _____
6. F _____
7. T _____
8. F _____
9. T _____
10. F _____
11. T _____
12. F _____
13. T _____
14. T _____
15. F _____
16. F _____
17. T _____
18. F _____
19. T _____
20. T _____
21. F _____
22. T _____
23. F _____
24. T _____
25. T _____
26. F _____
27. F _____
28. T _____
29. T _____
30. T _____

▲ FOLD FORWARD TO SCORE ▲

INTERPRETING YOUR SCORE

Low Scorers (0–12)—People who score low on this scale are often described by others as relaxed in social situations, dominant, and open to new experiences. If you scored in this range and feel comfortable that these adjectives describe you as you see yourself, that's great. You probably find it easy to take tests such as this one, unafraid of what the results will be. In fact, you may find pleasure in entering situations where others fear to tread, often having your own confidence serve as a model to encourage others.

Average Scorers (13–20)—The 33 percent of the people who score in this range are possibly seen by some as fearful of entering social-evaluative situations. Other people, however, may see you, if you scored here, as confident and unafraid of negative evaluation. The apparent paradox results from the situations themselves. As you look back over the items, think about any specific situations in which you particularly worry about negative evaluation. For example, at work you may be seen as a confident, risk-taking individual, while in social situations you may worry constantly about looking foolish. Different feelings in different situations, however, are normal and need not be a problem for you.

High Scorers (21–30)—People who score high on this scale are usually apprehensive about what other people think of them. This can cause less than enjoyable social and work relationships. As a high scorer, you probably find yourself quite distressed when negatively evaluated and often avoid situations where a negative evaluation is possible. This does not necessarily mean that you always evaluate yourself in a negative light, though that may be the unhappy companion of worrying about what others think of you. It does mean that, for some reason, you may have learned that acting defensive, subservient, and perhaps self-effacing is the best way to avoid having others criticize you. If these statements are true for you, taking this test and reading this interpretation of your score may have, unfortunately, confirmed your fears by presenting you with a negative evaluation. The fact that you did take this test and are reading this discussion suggests that you may be ready for some meaningful change in this part of your life.

ABOUT THE SCALE

Much of the anxiety and discomfort we feel results from how others treat us. But psychologists also know (probably to no one's surprise) that we also feel anxious worrying about how people *will* treat us *before* we interact with them. In essence, we anticipate the problem, and our anxiety level builds before the "real" problem is at hand.

You have no doubt been getting ready for something such as a job interview or a date and thought, "I just know I'll make a mess of things and an ass out of myself." You could close your eyes and visualize the upcoming mistakes you were certain that you would make. Your anxiety level began to build as you anticipated the problem situation; you got increasingly nervous, sweaty, overconcerned, and by the time the real situation occurred, the odds were great that your worst fears would come true.

After becoming aware of the need for a way to measure the anxiety related to such anticipated problems, psychologists David Watson and Ronald Friend developed the Fear of Negative Evaluation Scale. Such before-the-fact anxiety was defined by Drs. Watson and Friend as the apprehension you feel about going into a situation where you will be evaluated by another person. You will note from the test items that the other person does not need to be someone such as your boss or spouse but can be anyone who is in a position to say, "You're no good!" The scale also attempts to measure the likelihood that you will avoid such evaluative situations.

Hostility Inventory

by Arnold H. Buss
and Ann Durkee

Tear out the facing page labeled "Answer Sheet." Use this form for recording your answers to the sixty-six statements listed below and on the next page (after the answer sheet is torn out). Decide if each of the statements is true (T) or false (F) as it pertains to you and record your response in the appropriate box on the answer sheet. Note: A duplicate answer form is printed on the back of the answer sheet.

1. Unless somebody asks me in a nice way, I won't do what they want.
2. I don't seem to get what's coming to me.
3. I sometimes spread gossip about people I don't like.
4. Once in a while I cannot control my urge to harm others.
5. I know that people tend to talk about me behind my back.
6. I lose my temper easily but get over it quickly.
7. When I disapprove of my friends' behavior, I let them know it.
8. When someone makes a rule I don't like, I am tempted to break it.
9. Other people always seem to get the breaks.
10. I never get mad enough to throw things.
11. I can think of no good reason for ever hitting anyone.
12. I tend to be on my guard with people who are somewhat more friendly than I expected.
13. I am always patient with others.
14. I often find myself disagreeing with people.
15. When someone is bossy, I do the opposite of what he asks.
16. When I look back on what's happened to me, I can't help feeling mildly resentful.
17. When I am mad, I sometimes slam doors.
18. If somebody hits me first, I let him have it.
19. There are a number of people who seem to dislike me very much.
20. I am irritated a great deal more than people are aware of.
21. I can't help getting into arguments with people when they disagree with me.
22. When people are bossy, I take my time just to show them.
23. Almost every week I see someone I dislike.
24. I never play practical jokes.
25. Whoever insults me or my family is asking for a fight.

Buss, A. H., and Durkee, A. An inventory for assessing the different kinds of hostility. *Journal of Consulting Psychology*, 1957, 21, *4*, Table 1, p. 524. Copyright 1957 by the American Psychological Association. Reprinted by permission.

ANSWER SHEET

(Tear Out)

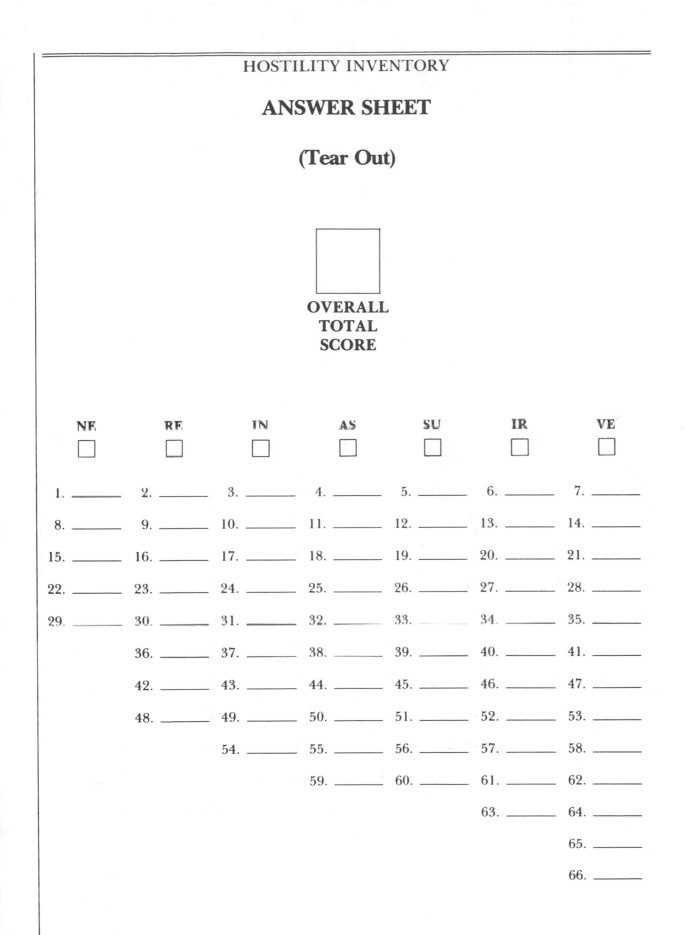

**OVERALL
TOTAL
SCORE**

NE	RE	IN	AS	SU	IR	VE
☐	☐	☐	☐	☐	☐	☐
1. ___	2. ___	3. ___	4. ___	5. ___	6. ___	7. ___
8. ___	9. ___	10. ___	11. ___	12. ___	13. ___	14. ___
15. ___	16. ___	17. ___	18. ___	19. ___	20. ___	21. ___
22. ___	23. ___	24. ___	25. ___	26. ___	27. ___	28. ___
29. ___	30. ___	31. ___	32. ___	33. ___	34. ___	35. ___
	36. ___	37. ___	38. ___	39. ___	40. ___	41. ___
	42. ___	43. ___	44. ___	45. ___	46. ___	47. ___
	48. ___	49. ___	50. ___	51. ___	52. ___	53. ___
		54. ___	55. ___	56. ___	57. ___	58. ___
			59. ___	60. ___	61. ___	62. ___
					63. ___	64. ___
						65. ___
						66. ___

ANSWER SHEET

(Tear Out)

**OVERALL
TOTAL
SCORE**

NE	RE	IN	AS	SU	IR	VE
☐	☐	☐	☐	☐	☐	☐

NE	RE	IN	AS	SU	IR	VE
1. _____	2. _____	3. _____	4. _____	5. _____	6. _____	7. _____
8. _____	9. _____	10. _____	11. _____	12. _____	13. _____	14. _____
15. _____	16. _____	17. _____	18. _____	19. _____	20. _____	21. _____
22. _____	23. _____	24. _____	25. _____	26. _____	27. _____	28. _____
29. _____	30. _____	31. _____	32. _____	33. _____	34. _____	35. _____
	36. _____	37. _____	38. _____	39. _____	40. _____	41. _____
	42. _____	43. _____	44. _____	45. _____	46. _____	47. _____
	48. _____	49. _____	50. _____	51. _____	52. _____	53. _____
		54. _____	55. _____	56. _____	57. _____	58. _____
			59. _____	60. _____	61. _____	62. _____
					63. _____	64. _____
						65. _____
						66. _____

26. There are a number of people who seem to be jealous of me.

27. It makes my blood boil to have somebody make fun of me.

28. I demand that people respect my rights.

29. Occasionally when I am mad at someone I will give him the "silent treatment."

30. Although I don't show it, I am sometimes eaten up with jealousy.

31. When I am angry, I sometimes sulk.

32. People who continually pester you are asking for a punch in the nose.

33. I sometimes have the feeling that others are laughing at me.

34. If someone doesn't treat me right, I don't let it annoy me.

35. Even when my anger is aroused, I don't use "strong language."

36. I don't know any people that I downright hate.

37. I sometimes pout when I don't get my own way.

38. I seldom strike back, even if someone hits me first.

39. My motto is "Never trust strangers."

40. Sometimes people bother me by just being around.

41. If somebody annoys me, I am apt to tell him what I think of him.

42. If I let people see the way I feel, I'd be considered a hard person to get along with.

43. Since the age of ten, I have never had a temper tantrum.

44. When I really lose my temper, I am capable of slapping someone.

45. I commonly wonder what hidden reason another person may have for doing something nice for me.

46. I often feel like a powder keg ready to explode.

47. When people yell at me, I yell back.

48. At times I feel I get a raw deal out of life.

49. I can remember being so angry that I picked up the nearest thing and broke it.

50. I get into fights about as often as the next person.

51. I used to think that most people told the truth but now I know otherwise.

52. I sometimes carry a chip on my shoulder.

53. When I get mad, I say nasty things.

54. I sometimes show my anger by banging on the table.

55. If I have to resort to physical violence to defend my rights, I will.

56. I have no enemies who really wish to harm me.

57. I can't help being a little rude to people I don't like.

58. I could not put someone in his place, even if he needed it.

59. I have known people who pushed me so far that we came to blows.

60. I seldom feel that people are trying to anger or insult me.

61. I don't let a lot of unimportant things irritate me.

62. I often make threats I don't really mean to carry out.

63. Lately, I have been kind of grouchy.

64. When arguing, I tend to raise my voice.

65. I generally cover up my poor opinion of others.

66. I would rather concede a point than get into an argument about it.

SCORING THE INVENTORY

Compare your answers to those listed on the Scoring Key below. Each column on your answer sheet (and Scoring Key) represents a separate subscale of the Hostility Inventory. Mark those answers that *agree* with the ones listed on the Scoring Key. Then add each column separately and place the number of total agreements in the boxes at the top of each column. After you have done this for each of the seven columns, add across the boxes at the top of the page and place that number in the box marked "Overall Total Score."

SCORING KEY

NE	RE	IN	AS	SU	IR	VE
1. T	2. T	3. T	4. T	5. T	6. T	7. T
8. T	9. T	10. F	11. F	12. T	13. F	14. T
15. T	16. T	17. T	18. T	19. T	20. T	21. T
22. T	23. T	24. F	25. T	26. T	27. T	28. T
29. T	30. T	31. T	32. T	33. T	34. F	35. F
	36. F	37. T	38. F	39. T	40. T	41. T
	42. T	43. F	44. T	45. T	46. T	47. T
	48. T	49. T	50. T	51. T	52. T	53. T
		54. T	55. T	56. F	57. T	58. F
			59. T	60. F	61. F	62. T
					63. T	64. T
						65. F
						66. F

INTERPRETING YOUR SCORE

Hostility is often the by-product of frustration and the high stress levels that frustration can produce. Most of us are comfortable with different levels of our own hostile feelings, but for some, any hostile feelings at all may be too many to accept. Others may look at the scores we have listed below as high and regard such levels of hostility as necessary to making it through each day.

According to data collected by Drs. Buss and Durkee, most people score below 38 in terms of total hostility, with women scoring slightly lower than men. If your Overall Total Score is well above 38, you are probably already aware of your hostile feelings. Your hostility may make your daily life and various relationships difficult and unpleasant. Without some sincere self-examination, best assisted by professional help, you may find it difficult to lower your level of hostility, frustration, and stress.

Even if you obtained an overall score of less than 38, look over the seven categories and note what constitutes a high score for each of them. One or more of these areas could be a problem for you. Your score for each area is listed at the top of the seven columns on your answer sheet.

NE   NEGATIVISM
High Score: 4 and above

Negativism usually is oppositional behavior against authority. It involves refusing to cooperate and can be seen in behavior that can range from passive noncompliance to open rebellion against rules or conventions.

RE   RESENTMENT
High Score: 4 and above

Resentment involves being jealous of others, often to a level of hatred. It is often a feeling of anger at the world over real or imagined mistreatment.

IN   INDIRECT HOSTILITY
High Score: 6 and above

Indirect hostility involves behavior that directs hostility toward someone in a roundabout way. It can be devious in that, through malicious gossip or practical jokes, the hated person receives the hostility but cannot do much about it. Other indirect behaviors, such as door slamming and temper tantrums, allow a person to discharge general feelings of hostility that may not be directed against anyone in particular.

AS   ASSAULT
High Score: 6 and above

Assault involves actual physical violence and the willingness to use physical violence against others. It is usually seen in fights with other people rather than in the destruction of objects.

SU   SUSPICION
High Score: 4 and above

Suspicion involves the projection of hostility onto others. It can vary from being distrustful and wary of others to serious beliefs that other people are planning one harm.

IR   IRRITABILITY
High Score: 8 and above

Irritability is a readiness to explode at the slightest provocation. It may be seen in behaviors such as quick-temper outbursts, grouchiness, and rudeness.

VE   VERBAL HOSTILITY
High Score: 9 and above

Verbal hostility involves the expression of negative feelings verbally to others, both in what is said and in how it is said. It can be seen in the verbal styles of arguing, shouting, and screaming, and in the verbal content of threats, curses, and overcriticism.

ABOUT THE INVENTORY

You can use the word "hostile" to describe someone who has just beaten his wife or to describe an associate who is always just a little late for appointments with you. The term may apply equally well to those two people, but your feelings about them and their hostile behavior would not be equal. Such an observation led psychologists Arnold Buss and Ann Durkee to state, "The writers know of no published hostility inventory that attempts more than a global estimate of hostility." As clinical psychologists, their concern—and need—was to find a way to describe hostile behavior in detail, a technique that would allow the psychologist and the client a better analysis of the global term "hostility."

The first part of their work involved defining the types of hostility that they, as psychologists, saw in everyday clinical situations. Their efforts resulted in the seven categories discussed in the interpretation section. They then developed a large number of statements which represented behaviors and feelings for those subtypes of hostility. Subsequent research narrowed their initial group of items to the sixty-six used in this final form of the Hostility Inventory.

Self-Consciousness Scale

by Allan Fenigstein,
Michael Scheier, and Arnold Buss

Below are twenty-three statements that may or may not be characteristic of the way you see yourself as a person. Read each one carefully and rate whether the statement is characteristic or uncharacteristic of you using the rating scale in the next column. Place the number of your answer in the appropriate box.

Extremely uncharacteristic = 0
Generally uncharacteristic = 1
Equally characteristic and
    uncharacteristic = 2
Generally characteristic = 3
Extremely characteristic = 4

_____ 1. I'm always trying to figure myself out.

_____ 2. I'm concerned about my style of doing things.

_____ 3. Generally, I'm very aware of myself.

_____ 4. It takes me time to overcome my shyness in new situations.

_____ 5. I reflect about myself a lot.

_____ 6. I'm concerned about the way I present myself.

_____ 7. I'm often the subject of my own fantasies.

_____ 8. I have trouble working when someone is watching me.

_____ 9. I constantly scrutinize myself.

_____ 10. I get embarrassed very easily.

_____ 11. I'm self-conscious about the way I look.

_____ 12. I find it hard to talk to strangers.

_____ 13. I'm generally attentive to my inner feelings.

_____ 14. I usually worry about making a good impression.

_____ 15. I'm constantly examining my motives.

_____ 16. I feel anxious when I speak in front of a large group.

_____ 17. One of the last things I do before I leave the house is look in the mirror.

_____ 18. I sometimes have the feeling that I'm off somewhere watching myself.

_____ 19. I'm concerned about what other people think of me.

_____ 20. I'm alert to changes in my mood.

_____ 21. I'm usually aware of my appearance.

_____ 22. I'm aware of the way my mind works when I work through a problem.

_____ 23. Large groups make me nervous.

Fenigstein, A., Scheier, M., & Buss, A. "Public and private self-consciousness: Assessment and theory." *Journal of Consulting and Clinical Psychology*, 1975, *43*, Table 1, p. 524. Copyright 1975 by the American Pyschological Association. Reprinted by permission.

SCORING KEY

	A	B	C
1.	☐		
2.		☐	
3.	☐		
4.			☐
5.	☐		
6.		☐	
7.	☐		
8.			☐
9.	☐		
10.			☐
11.		☐	
12.			☐
13.	☐		
14.		☐	
15.	☐		
16.			☐
17.		☐	
18.	☐		
19.		☐	
20.	☐		
21.		☐	
22.	☐		
23.			☐

FOLD BACK TO SCORE

SCORING THE SCALE

To find your score, fold this page back along the dotted line and transfer your answers onto the Scoring Key. The spaces on the Scoring Key are arranged in three columns. Each of your answers will fall into only one of those columns. Each column represents one of the three sub-scales in the Self-Consciousness Scale.

To obtain your score for each set of items, add down the columns and place your total for each column in the appropriate boxes below. Then add those three scores together and place that number in the box marked "Overall Total Score." Your score for "A" can range from 0 to 40; for "B," from 0 to 28; for "C," from 0 to 24; and for "Overall Total," from 0 to 92.

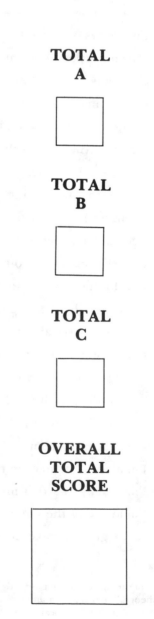

TOTAL A

☐

TOTAL B

☐

TOTAL C

☐

OVERALL TOTAL SCORE

☐

INTERPRETING YOUR SCORE

General Self-Consciousness. The average range for scores on the total Self-Consciousness Scale is from 53 to 63. People who score below this range tend not to spend much time or energy examining their own behavior or scrutinizing their thoughts. To other people, this may appear as a lack of self-understanding or as an unwillingness to be concerned about personal growth. High scorers focus on their own thoughts and actions much of the time and are concerned about the motives for their own behavior. At its extreme, self-consciousness can appear as an obsessiveness with self-examination.

A. *Private Self-Consciousness.* The average range for this subscale is from 23 to 29. Lower scorers show the tendency to avoid thinking about themselves and are reluctant to examine their own inner thoughts, feelings, and impulses. High scorers are very concerned about the "inner self" and spend high levels of energy in self-examination. In addition, high scorers are sensitive, perhaps overly sensitive, to events in their environment that affect them. A high level of private self-consciousness may be, for some, undesirable. Constant self-examining thoughts can inhibit the action needed to make the changes discovered during that period of reflection.

B. *Public Self-Consciousness.* The average range for this set of items is from 16 to 22. Low scorers show little concern about how other people will react to them in social settings. This may relate to a lack of awareness about how they appear to others or to an apparent insensitivity born out of high self-confidence. High scorers, on the other hand, are very concerned about the actions and opinions of others that relate to them. Such awareness may make one overly sensitive and highly susceptible to feelings of rejection.

C. *Social Anxiety.* The average range for this subscale is from 9 to 16. Low scorers generally appear confident in social situations and at ease when interacting with other people. High scorers show discomfort in such social situations. This anxiety may stem from self-examination that has left the person concerned about certain inadequacies. Since the danger in looking inward is that it could trigger feelings of anxiety, the socially anxious individual may begin to avoid social interactions altogether. These problems, however, will not change any more than the world of the ostrich changes while he has his head buried in the sand. High social anxiety needs and responds well to professional help.

ABOUT THE SCALE

Carl Jung developed the concept of introversion in 1933. G. H. Mead developed ideas about the impact of an individual becoming aware of himself as a social object in 1934. Psychologists Allan Fenigstein, Michael Scheier, and Arnold Buss unified these views to produce the Self-Consciousness Scale in 1975.

Basing their desire to develop a new measure of self-consciousness on Jung, Mead, and recent social psychological theory, these three psychologists divided that global concept into three subsets: private self-consciousness, public self-consciousness, and social anxiety. The first, private self-consciousness, is similar to Jung's idea about introversion. Both deal "with a cognitive, private mulling over the self." They emphasize internal experiences, known, perhaps, only to the individual himself. The second subscale, that of public self-consciousness, comes about, as Mead argued, "when the person becomes aware of another's perspective; then he can view himself as a social object." The emphasis in public self-consciousness is on how others react to us and to that part of us we consider *self*. Social anxiety, the third factor, is defined as a discomfort in the presence of others. According to Drs. Fenigstein, Scheier, and Buss, social anxiety may relate to a deficit in our ability to handle our public self-consciousness. Once we become aware of how others react to us, we may see ourselves as falling short of some ideal and become apprehensive. They point out, however, "self-awareness does not automatically imply social anxiety; a person may focus attention on himself without experiencing discomfort."

Moral Anxiety Questionnaire

by Lawrence R. Good and Katherine C. Good

Read the statements below and decide whether each is true (T) or false (F) for you. Try not to spend too long thinking about any of the statements. Mark your answer in the appropriate space for each one.

_____ 1. I sometimes worry that I may not be living up to the ethical standards I have set for myself.

_____ 2. I have a tendency to worry about not following the teachings of my religion as closely as I should.

_____ 3. I have a tendency to worry about having disappointed other people.

_____ 4. I sometimes worry that I may speak angrily to someone.

_____ 5. I sometimes worry that I may gossip about someone.

_____ 6. I sometimes worry that I may be receiving special privileges that are denied to others.

_____ 7. I sometimes worry about being more fortunate than someone else.

_____ 8. I have a tendency to worry that I may not be giving enough time to my schoolwork or to my job.

_____ 9. I have a tendency to worry that I may do things which are inconsiderate of other people's feelings.

_____ 10. I sometimes worry that I may not be giving enough time or attention to members of my family.

_____ 11. I sometimes worry that I may be too selfish or self-centered.

_____ 12. I sometimes worry about not always giving my help when it's asked for.

_____ 13. I sometimes worry that I may be taking advantage of someone else.

_____ 14. I have a tendency to worry that I may not love other members of my family as much as I should.

_____ 15. I sometimes worry about not being very cooperative.

_____ 16. I have a tendency to worry about things I have done in the past.

_____ 17. I sometimes worry that I may not do enough for others who are less fortunate than myself.

_____ 18. I sometimes worry about being too impatient with other people.

_____ 19. I have a tendency to worry about breaking a promise to someone.

_____ 20. I sometimes worry about feeling uncomfortable around handicapped or disabled people.

_____ 21. I sometimes worry about not being grateful enough for what I have.

_____ 22. I sometimes worry about having hostile feelings toward someone else.

_____ 23. I sometimes worry about not liking someone.

_____ 24. I sometimes worry that I may be causing hardship for someone else.

_____ 25. I sometimes worry that I may do things in the future that I will later be ashamed of.

_____ 26. I sometimes worry about being insincere.

_____ 27. I have a tendency to worry about being too harsh in my judgments of other people.

_____ 28. I sometimes worry about whether I am a worthwhile person.

_____ 29. I sometimes worry about behaving in an immature manner.

_____ 30. I sometimes worry about being too concerned with money or personal possessions.

_____ 31. I sometimes worry about being too greedy or ambitious.

_____ 32. I sometimes worry about acting rude or impolite toward others.

_____ 33. I sometimes worry about being too much of a pleasure seeker.

_____ 34. I sometimes worry that I may not be fulfilling all of my responsibilities.

SCORING THE QUESTIONNAIRE

Your score for the Moral Anxiety Questionnaire is the total number of times that you answered "true" for these statements. Place that number in the box labeled "Total Score." Your score on this questionnaire can range from 0 to 34.

TOTAL SCORE

INTERPRETING YOUR SCORE

As Sigmund Freud stated, some worry about doing what is morally right is necessary in social situations. Such worry helps us to be considerate and concerned about others in our society. Thus a very low level of moral anxiety (a score of 8 or less) may suggest an indifference to the needs of others, a kind of egoism and independence from concern about fellow human beings. At the other end of the continuum, however, a very high level of moral anxiety (scores of 22 or greater) may relate to an inability to relax and enjoy life. Someone that worried about violating moral principles may adopt a rigid, self-effacing approach to life. Worry may take so much energy that there may be little left for actual socially concerned behavior. Scores ranging from 9 to 21, the average, suggest a reasonable balance of independent motivation and socially responsible behavior.

ABOUT THE QUESTIONNAIRE

In 1933, Sigmund Freud divided his conceptualization of anxiety into three subdivisions: realistic anxiety, neurotic anxiety, and moral anxiety. We have discussed the qualities associated with the first two types in the introduction to this chapter. The third, moral anxiety, relates to that part of our personality Freud called the *superego*. The superego is often thought of today as being similar to the conscience in that it retains what we have learned in terms of social and moral rights and wrongs. According to Freud, the superego controls our behavior by allowing us to feel pride when we do something that our moral upbringing says is right or appropriate. But when we do something that our parents or our religious/social training says is wrong, the superego punishes us with feelings of guilt. It follows from this view of personality development that if we are fraught with worry about getting criticized by our superego, our conscience, we are then suffering moral anxiety.

Having feelings of moral anxiety is not, according to Freud, necessarily bad:

Fear of the superego should normally never cease since, in the form of moral anxiety, it is indispensable in social relations, and only in the rarest cases can an individual become independent of human society.

Psychologists Lawrence and Katherine Good decided to see if they could develop a measure of moral anxiety. The items in their questionnaire are intended to sample the kinds of situations where you may worry about doing what you have been taught is right. In Chapter One, you took the Crowne-Marlowe Social Desirability Scale. Questions on that scale asked you for what you *did* in certain social and moral situations. The Moral Anxiety Questionnaire, on the other hand, is concerned with your anxiety about the *possibility* of doing something wrong, even though you may act correctly all of the time.

Death Concern Scale

by Louis S. Dickstein

The Death Concern Scale contains 30 statements. Answer 1 through 11 using the answers "never" through "often," and their corresponding point values. Statements 12 through 30 are answered using the continuum of "I strongly agree" through "I strongly disagree," along with their corresponding point values. Place the number of your answer in the space provided for each statement on the answer sheet below. Try to answer using your first reaction to each item.

ANSWER SHEET

Never = 1 point

Rarely = 2 points

Sometimes = 3 points

Often = 4 points

I strongly agree = 1 point

I somewhat agree = 2 points

I somewhat disagree = 3 points

I strongly disagree = 4 points

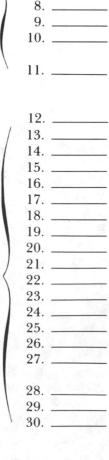

1. _____
2. _____
3. _____
4. _____
5. _____
6. _____
7. _____
8. _____
9. _____
10. _____
11. _____

12. _____
13. _____
14. _____
15. _____
16. _____
17. _____
18. _____
19. _____
20. _____
21. _____
22. _____
23. _____
24. _____
25. _____
26. _____
27. _____
28. _____
29. _____
30. _____

Reprinted with permission of author and publisher from: Dickstein, L. S. Death concern: Measurement and correlates. *Psychological Reports*, 1972, *30*, Table 1, p. 565.

1. I think about my own death.
2. I think about the death of loved ones.
3. I think about dying young.
4. I think about the possibility of my being killed on a city street.
5. I have fantasies of my own death.
6. I think about death just before I go to sleep.
7. I think of how I would act if I knew I were to die within a given period of time.
8. I think of how my relatives would act and feel upon my death.
9. When I am sick I think about death.
10. When I am outside during a lightning storm I think about the possibility of being struck by lightning.
11. When I am in an automobile I think about the high incidence of traffic fatalities.

12. I think people should first become concerned about death when they are old.
13. I am much more concerned about death than those around me.
14. Death hardly concerns me.
15. My general outlook just doesn't allow for morbid thoughts.
16. The prospect of my own death arouses anxiety in me.
17. The prospect of my own death depresses me.
18. The prospect of the death of my loved ones arouses anxiety in me.
19. The knowledge that I will surely die does not in any way affect the conduct of my life.
20. I envision my own death as a painful, nightmarish experience.
21. I am afraid of dying.
22. I am afraid of being dead.
23. Many people become disturbed at the sight of a new grave but it does not bother me.
24. I am disturbed when I think about the shortness of life.
25. Thinking about death is a waste of time.
26. Death should not be regarded as a tragedy if it occurs after a productive life.
27. The inevitable death of man poses a serious challenge to the meaningfulness of human existence.
28. The death of the individual is ultimately beneficial because it facilitates change in society.
29. I have a desire to live on after death.
30. The question of whether or not there is a future life worries me considerably.

SCORING KEY

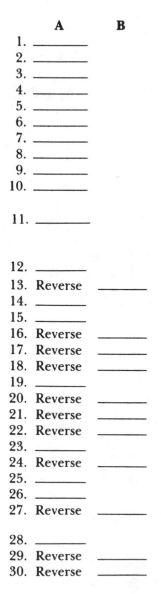

	A	B
1.	_____	
2.	_____	
3.	_____	
4.	_____	
5.	_____	
6.	_____	
7.	_____	
8.	_____	
9.	_____	
10.	_____	
11.	_____	
12.	_____	
13. Reverse	_____	
14.	_____	
15.	_____	
16. Reverse	_____	
17. Reverse	_____	
18. Reverse	_____	
19.	_____	
20. Reverse	_____	
21. Reverse	_____	
22. Reverse	_____	
23.	_____	
24. Reverse	_____	
25.	_____	
26.	_____	
27. Reverse	_____	
28.	_____	
29. Reverse	_____	
30. Reverse	_____	

FOLD BACK TO SCORE

SCORING THE SCALE

To find your score, fold the Scoring Key back along the dotted line and transfer your answers into Column A. Next, for items 13, 16, 17, 18, etc. *reverse the score* as shown below and enter it in Column B.

In Column B, an answer of

> 1 earns 4 points
> 2 earns 3 points
> 3 earns 2 points
> 4 earns 1 point

To find your final score, add together the total points in both columns and enter that number in the box below.

TOTAL SCORE

INTERPRETING YOUR SCORE

Low Scorers (30–67)—Low scorers are acknowledging little, if any, apprehension about death. For you, this may reflect a well-thought-out acceptance of your own mortality. Thus thinking about death does not produce much emotional discomfort. Or (psychologists are forever looking for the other side of the coin) your low score may indicate a defensive position about death. You may be reluctant to think about the possibility that you are not in total control of your life and could die, so refusing to think about death could serve as a defense against anxiety. Only you can decide which is the more accurate interpretation of your score.

Average Scorers (68–80)—People who score in this range do have higher concerns about death than do low scorers. But average scorers do not show overall high anxiety levels as is characteristic of high scorers. Perhaps you scored in this range because personal experi-

ences have sensitized you to the topic of death. Average scorers do tend to be more sensitive to what is going on around them than people in the lower range of scores.

High Scorers (81–120)—Just looking at the title of this scale was probably enough to increase your anxiety level. As a high scorer, you are reporting much concern about death and are likely to be very sensitive whenever the topic is mentioned. A more bothersome problem for you, however, may be an overall high level of "free-floating" anxiety, with death only one of many topics that stimulate strong feelings of anxiety. High scorers are often seen as showing a desire for help and encouragement, sympathy, and understanding. If this describes you, professional help may be just the thing to help you make your life more relaxed and enjoyable.

ABOUT THE SCALE

You have heard the old saying, "Only two things in life are certain, death and taxes." As far as we know, psychologists have not yet designed a test to measure anxiety over taxes. But psychologists have, for several years, been focusing on death as a topic and on the anxiety that thinking about death produces.

Though anxiety is often thought of as "free-floating" and nebulous, death—the word and the process—is an anxiety-provoking topic for many of us. Our intellectual capabilities cannot deal with their own nonexistence. It is impossible, and perhaps frightening, to contemplate what death is like. After all, the bad guy on TV gets killed one week and appears on a soap commercial the next. But for many, concern about the potential personal reality of death produces high levels of anxiety.

Wellesley College psychologist Louis Dickstein began his efforts to measure such death concern in the mid-1960s. His work led him to write in 1972:

Despite the fact that there has been a steady increase in interest in the psychology of death over the past decade, research has been hampered by the absence of reliable and valid methods for the measurement of concern about death.

Dr. Dickstein saw the need for a well-thought-out scale, one that could use as its basis, a test that he and Dr. Sidney Blatt developed in 1966. The Death Concern Scale which we have included here is the result of that effort.

CHAPTER FOUR

Fear

"*O*f all the bad passions fear is the most accursed," wrote William Shakespeare half a millennium before Freud. Anger can be a nightmarish emotion but at least in most instances you have the opportunity to approach the source of your anger and confront it. With fear, your only escape from the feeling is to run away or retreat into yourself. In grief, there may sometimes be found deep meaning. In shame, one might find the path to self-improvement. Fear in its mild form—roller coasters, horror movies—can be thrilling, but moderate to intense fear can be emotionally and physically debilitating.

The physical symptoms of intense fear—dry mouth, rapid pulse, cold sweat, shivering—go back to our evolutionary origins when the flight or fight reaction evolved. If it were not for the hormones which elicit such unpleasant reactions, our forebears might have been eaten by the competition, and we wouldn't be here today to talk about it. Even though we live in a vastly changed environment, our bodies tend to react to threatening stimuli in the same way they did back on the primordial savannah.

It is in the higher centers of the brain, where creativity and imagination are operative, that the modern problems with fear reside. Our fearful responses may be innate, and certain fears—fear of falling, for example—may also be biologically "wired in," but most of the objects or situations that trigger many of these responses are for the most part *learned*. In general these emotions are useful—we do not step into the path of speeding autos, and we do keep our fingers away from hot stoves. In some cases, however, totally irrational fears can be picked up through social learning and classical conditioning. In extreme cases, such fears can be paralyzing.

Agoraphobia—fear of the outside, of unbounded spaces, literally "fear of the marketplace"—is virtually a hidden plague. Thousands of people are confined to their homes because of their overwhelming fear of going outside. One man, to take a radical example, had to get his morning paper off his own doorstep by *backing* out the door—so he wouldn't have to face the outside world, and so he could run back inside very quickly. Other specific fears such as claustrophobia (fear of enclosed spaces) or acrophobia (fear of heights) prevent people from riding in elevators, automobiles, or airplanes. For those afflicted by highly specific phobias, there is now hope in the form of behavioral therapies such as systematic desensitization.

Before any therapeutic measures can be taken, or before anyone can learn to deal with his or her own fears, those fears must be uncovered. Our natural tendency is to cover up, repress, or avoid those things that we fear the most. This tendency makes testing a valuable tool for self-knowledge. Since fear of the unknown is an important component in almost every kind of fear, simply learning about one's fears can be a very useful, perhaps crucial, step toward managing those emotions.

Fear Survey Schedule II

by James H. Geer

Listed below are fifty-one objects and situations. Using the scoring system below, rate each on the intensity of your fear associated with that specific object or event.

1	2	3	4	5	6	7
NO FEAR	VERY LITTLE FEAR	A LITTLE FEAR	SOME FEAR	MUCH FEAR	GREAT FEAR	TERROR

_____ 1. Sharp objects
_____ 2. Being a passenger in a car
_____ 3. Dead bodies
_____ 4. Suffocating
_____ 5. Failing a test
_____ 6. Looking foolish
_____ 7. Being a passenger in an airplane
_____ 8. Worms
_____ 9. Arguing with parents
_____ 10. Rats and mice
_____ 11. Life after death
_____ 12. Hypodermic needles
_____ 13. Being criticized
_____ 14. Meeting someone for the first time
_____ 15. Roller coasters
_____ 16. Being alone
_____ 17. Making mistakes
_____ 18. Being misunderstood
_____ 19. Death
_____ 20. Being in a fight
_____ 21. Crowded places
_____ 22. Blood
_____ 23. Heights
_____ 24. Being a leader
_____ 25. Swimming alone
_____ 26. Illness

_____ 27. Being with drunks
_____ 28. Illness or injury to loved one
_____ 29. Being self-conscious
_____ 30. Driving a car
_____ 31. Meeting authority
_____ 32. Mental illness
_____ 33. Closed places
_____ 34. Boating
_____ 35. Spiders
_____ 36. Thunderstorms
_____ 37. Not being a success
_____ 38. God
_____ 39. Snakes
_____ 40. Cemeteries
_____ 41. Speaking before a group
_____ 42. Seeing a fight
_____ 43. Death of a loved one
_____ 44. Dark places
_____ 45. Strange dogs
_____ 46. Deep water
_____ 47. Being with a member of the opposite sex
_____ 48. Stinging insects
_____ 49. Untimely or early death
_____ 50. Losing a job
_____ 51. Auto accidents

Reprinted with permission from *Behavior Research and Therapy*, 1965, *3*, J. H. Geer, "The development of a scale to measure fear." Copyright 1965, Pergamon Press, Ltd.

SCORING THE SCHEDULE

Your total score for the Fear Survey Schedule II can be obtained by adding the numbers for each of the 51 items. Place that score in the box labeled "Total Score" below.

TOTAL SCORE

INTERPRETING YOUR SCORE

Dr. Geer's research found these fears (not necessarily in this order) as the twelve getting the highest intensity ratings:

4 Suffocating
5 Failing a test
6 Looking foolish
17 Making mistakes
28 Illness or injury to loved ones
29 Being self-conscious
37 Not being a success
39 Snakes
41 Speaking before a group
43 Death of a loved one
49 Untimely or early death

Women and men generally report being afraid of the same objects and situations. The intensity of those fears, however, is much higher for women than for men. On the Fear Survey Schedule II, the average overall intensity score for women is 100, with an average range of 82 to 118. For men the average intensity score is 75, with an average range of 58 to 93.

Psychologists find it much easier to describe people who score high on a test such as this one than those who score low. Low scorers just don't seem to have many fears and are not too intense about the ones they do have (granted that even low scorers may have one specific phobia that rates an intensity level of "Terror"). High scorers, on the other hand, tend to be generally anxious people, probably regarding themselves as highly emotional, perhaps to the point of sometimes feeling neurotic. If you scored above the average range for your sex, you didn't need this list to point out your level of fear. But the survey can help you quantify and focus that intensity on its true objects and situations. Treatment for such specific fears is the most effective type of therapy practiced by psychologists and psychiatrists. Life will seem brighter and less frightening if you will take advantage of that professional help.

ABOUT THE SURVEY

The concept of fear plays an important role in most personality theories. Psychologists attribute much of our waking as well as dreaming behavior to how we handle our fears and anxieties. Sigmund Freud's views on the unconscious mind stressed the importance of fear in the operation of what he termed "defense mechanisms." Defense mechanisms are those processes which repress or remove from our awareness our fear of specific objects and situations. Dreams were seen by Carl Jung as stimulated and shaped by that which we feared but could not handle during our waking time.

Given the central role that fear plays in explaining and directing our behavior, it is helpful to look at what it is that we do fear. With such an examination in mind, psychologist James Geer asked 124 research subjects to list their fears on an open-ended questionnaire. Out of the 111 different fears they listed, 51 occurred two or more times. Dr. Geer then developed these 51 into the Fear Survey Schedule II we have included here. His subsequent research with an additional 600 people enabled him to develop norms for what it is that people fear most and gain an overview of how intense those fears are.

It is certainly true that many more than these 51 items stimulate fear. Psychiatrists and psychologists have specifically labeled over 700 things to dread and estimate that there are thousands of phobias among us. For now, however, content yourself with worrying about these 51.

Dental Anxiety Scale

by Norman L. Corah

Below are four multiple-choice questions which deal with going to the dentist. Read each question and select whichever one of the answers best describes your feelings. Place the letter of your answer in the space next to each question. Take the test before reading further.

_____ 1. If you had to go to the dentist tomorrow, how would you feel about it?
   (a) I would look forward to it as a reasonably enjoyable experience
   (b) I wouldn't care one way or the other
   (c) I would be a little uneasy about it
   (d) I would be afraid that it would be unpleasant and painful
   (e) I would be very frightened of what the dentist might do

_____ 2. When you are waiting in the dentist's office for your turn in the chair, how do you feel?
   (a) Relaxed
   (b) A little uneasy
   (c) Tense
   (d) Anxious
   (e) So anxious that I sometimes break out in a sweat or almost feel physically sick

_____ 3. When you are in the dentist's chair waiting while he gets his drill ready to begin working on your teeth, how do you feel?
   (a) Relaxed
   (b) A little uneasy
   (c) Tense
   (d) Anxious
   (e) So anxious that I sometimes break out in a sweat or almost feel physically sick

_____ 4. You are in the dentist's chair to have your teeth cleaned. While you are waiting and the dentist is getting out the instruments which he will use to scrape your teeth around the gums, how do you feel?
   (a) Relaxed
   (b) A little uneasy
   (c) Tense
   (d) Anxious
   (e) So anxious that I sometimes break out in a sweat or almost feel physically sick

N. L. Corah, "Development of a dental anxiety scale," *Journal of Dental Research*, 1969, *48*, p. 596. Copyright 1969 by the American Association for Dental Research. Reprinted with permission.

SCORING THE SCALE

Compute your total score by giving yourself points on the following basis:

a = 1 point

b = 2 points

c = 3 points

d = 4 points

e = 5 points

Add the points for each of the four questions and put that total in the box provided.

TOTAL SCORE

INTERPRETING YOUR SCORE

Low Scorers (4–7)—Low scorers on this scale were raised well as children (at least in terms of visits to the dentist). They acknowledge little anxiety about having dental work done and are probably ideal patients. Their only problem may be trying to understand why some of their friends are so terrorized by the thought of visiting the dentist.

Average Scorers (8–12)—Average scorers express some apprehension about visits to the dentist but probably have it fairly well under control. They know that it's something that has to be done, but they do feel a bit squeamish about going. If you are an average scorer, you have probably developed some personal system to help you make it through your visit and reduce your uneasiness. Some people like to feel in control of the drilling—raise one finger to get it stopped. For others, concentration on the music, the nurse, or the dentist's glasses helps reduce the anxiety to a tolerable level.

High Scorers (13–20)—If you scored in this range, our best advice is to brush and floss regularly and avoid sweets. You don't like going to the dentist. In fact, if you scored 17 or above, you could be described as having a dental phobia. Admitting your fear is an excellent start. Many people are too embarrassed to admit to high dental fear since they know, rationally, that there is little to actually fear. Your fear level, however, either keeps you away from the dentist (causing unknown dental problems and increased anxiety over those) or takes you to the dentist in a state of extreme anxiety and stress. In either case, successful prevention or treatment of any dental problem will be difficult. Confronting your fear (with dental and psychological help, if necessary) may save you countless hours of anxiety—and your teeth as well.

ABOUT THE SCALE

The fear of going to the dentist is one of the most prominent fears in Western society. More than 100 million people in the United States fail to go to the dentist for regular checkups. Ten million of these people say that they are too afraid to go, according to an American Dental Association Survey. Even many of those who finally make it to the dentist are anxious and fearful from the time the nurse calls to confirm the appointment. The fear increases as the dreaded day—and drill—draw closer.

Psychologists and dentists alike, however, say that such fear is unnecessary. Dental technology has made major advances in reducing pain and discomfort. Effective local anesthetics, nitrous oxide, headphones and music, and even games of video pong are now part of the dentist's repertoire. Yet dental fear appears to be as prevalent today as it was fifteen years ago.

It was about that time that psychologist Norman Corah became aware of the pervasive nature of dental fears. He had used a video simulation of a dental procedure to induce psychological stress for a research project and was impressed by the intensity of the anxiety the film could produce. This led directly to his work to develop a formal measure of dental anxiety. Dr. Corah's goal was to provide the practicing dentist with a way to measure the patient's feelings about the upcoming treatment. He wrote, "If the dentist is aware of the level of anxiety of his patient, he is not only forewarned, but can also take measures to help alleviate the anxiety during the operative procedure." His Dental Anxiety Scale allows the dentist to gain that information through a set of questions that the patient answers while sitting in the waiting room. The scale can be scored and the results made available to the dentist before the patient has finished his *Reader's Digest*.

Anxiety Questionnaires

by Peter J. Lang

Beginning below are three questionnaires, ninety items in all, regarding your feelings about snakes, public speaking, and mutilation. Each statement can be answered either true (T) or false (F). To take the test, tear out the answer sheet on the next page and use it to record your answers. Try to answer using your first impression in deciding whether each statement is true or false for you. A duplicate of the answer sheet is printed on the back.

SNAKE ANXIETY QUESTIONNAIRE

by Peter J. Lang

_____ 1. I avoid going to parks or on camping trips because there may be snakes about.

_____ 2. I would feel some anxiety holding a toy snake in my hand.

_____ 3. If a picture of a snake appears on the screen during a motion picture I turn my head away.

_____ 4. I dislike looking at pictures of snakes in a magazine.

_____ 5. Although it may not be so, I think of snakes as slimy.

_____ 6. I enjoy watching snakes at the zoo.

_____ 7. I am terrified by the thought of touching a harmless snake.

_____ 8. If someone says that there are snakes anywhere about, I become alert and on edge.

_____ 9. I would not go swimming at the beach if snakes had ever been reported in the area.

_____ 10. I would feel uncomfortable wearing a snakeskin belt.

_____ 11. When I see a snake, I feel tense and restless.

_____ 12. I enjoy reading articles about snakes and other reptiles.

_____ 13. I feel sick when I see a snake.

_____ 14. Snakes are sometimes useful.

_____ 15. I shudder when I think of snakes.

_____ 16. I don't mind being near a nonpoisonous snake if there is someone there in whom I have confidence.

_____ 17. Some snakes are very attractive to look at.

_____ 18. I don't believe anyone could hold a snake without some fear.

_____ 19. The way snakes move is repulsive.

_____ 20. It wouldn't bother me to touch a dead snake with a long stick.

_____ 21. If I came upon a snake in the woods I would probably run.

_____ 22. I'm more afraid of snakes than any other animal.

_____ 23. I would not want to travel "down south" or in tropical countries, because of the greater prevalence of snakes.

_____ 24. I wouldn't take a course like biology if I thought you might have to dissect a snake.

_____ 25. I have no fear of nonpoisonous snakes.

_____ 26. Not only am I afraid of snakes, but worms and most reptiles make me feel anxious.

_____ 27. Snakes are very graceful animals.

_____ 28. I think that I am no more afraid of snakes than the average person.

_____ 29. I would prefer not to finish a story if something about snakes was introduced into the plot.

_____ 30. Even if I was late for a very important appointment, the thought of snakes would stop me from taking a shortcut through an open field.

ANSWER SHEET
(Tear Out)

SQ	PRCPS	MQ
1. _____	31. _____	61. _____
2. _____	32. _____	62. _____
3. _____	33. _____	63. _____
4. _____	34. _____	64. _____
5. _____	35. _____	65. _____
6. _____	36. _____	66. _____
7. _____	37. _____	67. _____
8. _____	38. _____	68. _____
9. _____	39. _____	69. _____
10. _____	40. _____	70. _____
11. _____	41. _____	71. _____
12. _____	42. _____	72. _____
13. _____	43. _____	73. _____
14. _____	44. _____	74. _____
15. _____	45. _____	75. _____
16. _____	46. _____	76. _____
17. _____	47. _____	77. _____
18. _____	48. _____	78. _____
19. _____	49. _____	79. _____
20. _____	50. _____	80. _____
21. _____	51. _____	81. _____
22. _____	52. _____	82. _____
23. _____	53. _____	83. _____
24. _____	54. _____	84. _____
25. _____	55. _____	85. _____
26. _____	56. _____	86. _____
27. _____	57. _____	87. _____
28. _____	58. _____	88. _____
29. _____	59. _____	89. _____
30. _____	60. _____	90. _____

TOTAL SCORE

TOTAL SCORE

TOTAL SCORE

ANSWER SHEET
(Tear Out)

SQ	PRCPS	MQ
1. _____	31. _____	61. _____
2. _____	32. _____	62. _____
3. _____	33. _____	63. _____
4. _____	34. _____	64. _____
5. _____	35. _____	65. _____
6. _____	36. _____	66. _____
7. _____	37. _____	67. _____
8. _____	38. _____	68. _____
9. _____	39. _____	69. _____
10. _____	40. _____	70. _____
11. _____	41. _____	71. _____
12. _____	42. _____	72. _____
13. _____	43. _____	73. _____
14. _____	44. _____	74. _____
15. _____	45. _____	75. _____
16. _____	46. _____	76. _____
17. _____	47. _____	77. _____
18. _____	48. _____	78. _____
19. _____	49. _____	79. _____
20. _____	50. _____	80. _____
21. _____	51. _____	81. _____
22. _____	52. _____	82. _____
23. _____	53. _____	83. _____
24. _____	54. _____	84. _____
25. _____	55. _____	85. _____
26. _____	56. _____	86. _____
27. _____	57. _____	87. _____
28. _____	58. _____	88. _____
29. _____	59. _____	89. _____
30. _____	60. _____	90. _____

TOTAL SCORE

TOTAL SCORE

TOTAL SCORE

PERSONAL REPORT OF CONFIDENCE AS A PUBLIC SPEAKER

by Peter J. Lang
after Gordon L. Paul

_____ 31. I look forward to an opportunity to speak in public.

_____ 32. My hands tremble when I try to handle objects on the platform.

_____ 33. I am in constant fear of forgetting my speech.

_____ 34. Audiences seem friendly when I address them.

_____ 35. While preparing a speech I am in a constant state of anxiety.

_____ 36. At the conclusion of a speech I feel that I have had a pleasant experience.

_____ 37. I dislike to use my body and voice expressively.

_____ 38. My thoughts become confused and jumbled when I speak before an audience.

_____ 39. I have no fear of facing an audience.

_____ 40. Although I am nervous just before getting up I soon forget my fears and enjoy the experience.

_____ 41. I face the prospect of making a speech with complete confidence.

_____ 42. I feel that I am in complete possession of myself while speaking.

_____ 43. I prefer to have notes on the platform in case I forget my speech.

_____ 44. I like to observe the reactions of my audience to my speech.

_____ 45. Although I talk fluently with friends I am at a loss for words on the platform.

_____ 46. I feel relaxed and comfortable while speaking.

_____ 47. Although I do not enjoy speaking in public I do not particularly dread it.

_____ 48. I always avoid speaking in public if possible.

_____ 49. The faces of my audience are blurred when I look at them.

_____ 50. I feel disgusted with myself after trying to address a group of people.

_____ 51. I enjoy preparing a talk.

_____ 52. My mind is clear when I face an audience.

_____ 53. I am fairly fluent.

_____ 54. I perspire and tremble just before getting up to speak.

_____ 55. My posture feels strained and unnatural.

_____ 56. I am fearful and tense all the while I am speaking before a group of people.

_____ 57. I find the prospect of speaking mildly pleasant.

_____ 58. It is difficult for me to calmly search my mind for the right words to express my thoughts.

_____ 59. I am terrified at the thought of speaking before a group of people.

_____ 60. I have a feeling of alertness in facing an audience.

MUTILATION QUESTIONNAIRE

by Peter J. Lang

_____ 61. I could not remove the hook from a fish that was caught.

_____ 62. I would feel some revulsion looking at a preserved brain in a bottle.

_____ 63. If a badly injured person appears on TV, I turn my head away.

_____ 64. I dislike looking at pictures of accidents or injuries in magazines.

_____ 65. I do not mind visiting a hospital and seeing ill or injured persons.

_____ 66. Medical odors make me tense and uncomfortable.

_____ 67. I would not go hunting because I could not stand the sight of a dead animal.

_____ 68. Watching a butcher at work would make me anxious.

_____ 69. A career as a doctor or nurse is very attractive to me.

_____ 70. I would feel faint if I saw someone with a wound in the eye.

_____ 71. Watching people use sharp power tools makes me nervous.

_____ 72. The prospect of getting an injection or seeing someone else get one bothers me quite a bit.

_____ 73. I feel sick or faint at the sight of blood.

_____ 74. I enjoy reading articles about modern medical techniques.

_____ 75. Injuries, accidents, blood, etc., bother me more than anything else.

_____ 76. Under no circumstances would I accept an invitation to watch a surgical operation.

_____ 77. When I see an accident I feel tense.

_____ 78. It would not bother me to see a bad cut as long as it had been cleaned and stitched.

_____ 79. Using very sharp knives makes me nervous.

_____ 80. Not only do cuts and wounds upset me, but the sight of people with amputated limbs, large scars, or plastic surgery also bothers me.

_____ 81. If instruments were available, it would be interesting to see the actions of the internal organs in a living body.

_____ 82. I am frightened at the idea of someone drawing a blood sample from me.

_____ 83. I don't believe anyone could help a person with a bloody wound without feeling at least a little upset.

_____ 84. I am terrified by the idea of having surgery.

_____ 85. I am frightened by the thought that I might someday have to help a person badly hurt in a car wreck.

_____ 86. I shudder when I think of accidentally cutting myself.

_____ 87. The sight of dried blood is repulsive.

_____ 88. Blood and gore upset me no more than the average person.

_____ 89. The sight of an open wound nauseates me.

_____ 90. I could never swab out a wound.

ABOUT THE QUESTIONNAIRE

Even the most normal of us is afraid of something. There are thousands of different objects and situations that have been classified as fear-producing. Some of us are afraid of heights *(acrophobia)*, others are afraid of depths *(bathophobia);* some are afraid of open places *(agoraphobia)*, others of closed ones *(claustrophobia)*. Some of us are afraid of ourselves *(monophobia)*, while others are afraid of everyone else *(anthrophobia)*. The list goes on and on, even to the point of our being afraid of everything *(pantophobia)*.

No one knows exactly why we develop the fears that we have. Some psychologists have argued that humans, like other animals, are innately "prepared" to learn to fear some things more than others. Our ancestors needed to be afraid of snakes, spiders, and disease-carrying rats. Fearing, or being prepared to fear, such animals may still be in our DNA, passed down from generation to generation. Other psychologists believe that fears are learned, either through direct experience or from observing the fear reactions of someone else.

Measuring how afraid someone is of any specific object or situation, however, is not an easy task. Psychologists such as Peter Lang have proposed a three-part model of fear which includes motor activity, physiological responses, and cognitive processes. If you were afraid of snakes, for example, we could observe your motor activity—running away from a snake, or a lack of movement toward somewhere a snake might be—and make a judgment about your fear of snakes. We could also measure your physiological responses—your heart rate, blood pressure, or palm sweating—and assess your fear level. But, as Dr. Lang and others have pointed out, there is also a large thinking, or cognitive, component to our fears. What you think about a certain situation, such as speaking in front of a group, could make it either a comfortable experience or a terrifying one. Should you decide that you are afraid, you will likely decide to avoid the object or event. It follows that the only way someone could tell that you were afraid of that situation would be to ask you for your thoughts and feelings about it.

The three questionnaires we have included here are based on that cognitive method of measuring fear. Each is a series of statements about feelings and thoughts related to either snakes, public speaking, or mutilation. The Snake Anxiety Questionnaire and the Mutilation Questionnaire were developed by Dr. Lang and several of his colleagues as part of a research program. The Personal Report of Confidence As a Public Speaker was developed by Dr. Gordon Paul and modified by Dr. Lang.

SCORING THE QUESTIONNAIRES

To find your score on the three questionnaires, compare your answers to the Scoring Key below. Give yourself one point for each matching answer. Add up each of the three columns separately and write your totals in the appropriate boxes on the answer sheet.

1. T _____	31. F _____	61. T _____
2. T _____	32. T _____	62. T _____
3. T _____	33. T _____	63. T _____
4. T _____	34. F _____	64. T _____
5. T _____	35. T _____	65. F _____
6. F _____	36. F _____	66. T _____
7. T _____	37. T _____	67. T _____
8. T _____	38. T _____	68. T _____
9. T _____	39. F _____	69. F _____
10. T _____	40. F _____	70. T _____
11. T _____	41. F _____	71. T _____
12. F _____	42. F _____	72. T _____
13. T _____	43. T _____	73. T _____
14. F _____	44. F _____	74. F _____
15. T _____	45. T _____	75. T _____
16. F _____	46. F _____	76. T _____
17. F _____	47. F _____	77. T _____
18. T _____	48. T _____	78. F _____
19. T _____	49. T _____	79. T _____
20. F _____	50. T _____	80. T _____
21. T _____	51. F _____	81. F _____
22. T _____	52. F _____	82. T _____
23. T _____	53. F _____	83. T _____
24. T _____	54. T _____	84. T _____
25. F _____	55. T _____	85. T _____
26. T _____	56. T _____	86. T _____
27. F _____	57. F _____	87. T _____
28. F _____	58. T _____	88. F _____
29. T _____	59. T _____	89. T _____
30. T _____	60. F _____	90. T _____

INTERPRETING YOUR SCORE

Otherwise healthy and relaxed individuals can score high on any one these questionnaires. What turns a fear into a problem is how we handle—or rather how we fail to handle—that fear. For example, someone who lives in a large metropolitan area could be cognitively terrified of snakes and never show any anxiety about them. If that same individual were to move to a rural river town, however, that same fear of snakes could become debilitating. The same general idea holds true for mutilation anxiety and a fear of public speaking. The fear only becomes a problem when the individual must make major, undesirable, or inconvenient life-style changes because of that fear.

As you interpret your own scores, consider how your fear, if you have one, affects your life. If it is forcing you into a living pattern that you don't want, then it is time for you to work on getting rid of that fear. The psychological techniques for fear reduction are relatively quick, effective, and generally more relaxing than disturbing.

Snake Anxiety Questionnaire. High Scorers (men, 8 and above; women, 12 and above)—As you can see, women generally score higher on this fear than men. During the Victorian era of Sigmund Freud, snake phobia took on heavily sexual interpretations. Freud saw the snake as the unconscious representation of the male sexual organ. A woman's fear of snakes was interpreted, as you can imagine, as a fear of sex or as a desire to possess a penis and be a man. For the man, snake phobia could represent his castration fears, the fear of losing his penis and, with it, his manhood. Carl Jung in his philosophical break with Freud viewed the snake as a symbol of the human's internal struggles. In keeping with his strongly religious orientation, Jung interpreted the snake's presence in our dreams and fears as representing the attempt of the shadow, our hidden evil side, to break into consciousness and into control of our personalities.

If you scored high on this questionnaire, you can start by setting up your own desensitization program. Get yourself as relaxed as possible, and picture a snake in your mind. At first, imagine the snake far away; then, as you continue relaxing, picture the snake coming closer, but only a little closer at a time. You might also look at a picture of a snake in a book, relaxing as much as possible while looking at the picture. If these first steps do not generate intolerable anxiety, you may be ready for a trip to a taxidermy shop for a look at a stuffed snake, gradually building your courage for a trip to your local zoo's reptile house. If your anxiety keeps you from even attempting such a self-help program, however, a professional therapist is your answer. Relaxation-desensitization programs for snake phobia are highly effective and may last for no more than six to ten weeks.

Personal Report of Confidence as a Public Speaker. High Scorers (22 and above)—Fear of speaking in front of groups is a common phobia. Many famous and successful actors, politicians, and sports personalities have written about their strong fears of getting up to talk to a group. In effect, they dealt with their fear by actively confronting it and thus building a financially and emotionally rewarding career out of a phobia. A fear of public speaking may

be one phobia learned in childhood. Parental pressure to perform, one bad subsequent presentation experience (or the observation of someone else's anxiety over his presentation), and a phobia such as this one is easily established.

If you scored high on this scale, you may find this fear interfering with various parts of your life. A fear of public speaking may reduce your job options, make it uncomfortable for you to attend social functions, or decrease your self-esteem. Such a fear is often difficult to work on by yourself, although you can start by using imagery and relaxation as discussed above for snake phobia. You could begin by relaxing and speaking to yourself in a mirror, then imagining yourself in situations involving increasing numbers of people. For the fastest and most effective way to reduce this fear, however, see a therapist.

Mutilation Questionnaire. High Scorers (men, 12 and above; women, 16 and above)—As with the fear of snakes, it is more common for women to be afraid of mutilation and blood than it is for men to show this fear. Perhaps "acknowledge the fear" would be a better term to describe the difference between the sexes. Many women were raised with the stereotype of being weak, which included fainting at the sight of blood, whereas men are pushed to cognitively ignore pain and suffering. Yet women seem to possess a stronger constitution when it comes to dealing with tragedy and pain. What we may be seeing on a psychological test such as this one is a response based on what people have been taught to say. If you scored high on this scale, it would be interesting for you to think about how your motor activity and physiological processes match your cognitive responses regarding this fear. In other words, when you are in a traumatic situation, how do you *really* react?

You can work to reduce this fear by arranging a desensitization program as discussed above for snake phobia. Relax and imagine situations involving only a little pain and blood. Once you handle the imagery of those, increase the degree of blood present in the imagined scenes, all the while remaining as relaxed as you can. For real-life practice, you could visit your butcher and watch some meat cutting or look through books that discuss related subjects. As with other fears, however, self-help programs may not work as well or as fast as you would like. In that case, professional help is your best alternative.

Reducer-Augmenter Scale

by Alan Vando

Below you will find a series of paired statements which you are asked to regard as choices. In some cases you will like both choices. In some cases you will dislike both choices. In other cases you will find the choices neutral. No matter how the items strike you, you are to quickly choose which of the alternatives you prefer in comparison to the other alternative. Tear out the answer sheet on the facing page to record your answers. A duplicate of the answer sheet is printed on the back.

1. a. see a war drama
   b. see a situation comedy

2. a. play sports requiring endurance
   b. play games with rest stops

3. a. raunchy blues
   b. straight ballads

4. a. jazz combo
   b. 1001 strings

5. a. stereo on too loud
   b. stereo on too low

6. a. own a goldfish
   b. own a turtle

7. a. conservatism
   b. militantism

8. a. too much sleep
   b. too little sleep

9. a. danger
   b. domesticity

10. a. passenger car
    b. sports car

11. a. have several pets
    b. have one pet

12. a. be a shepherd
    b. be a cowboy

13. a. motor scooter
    b. motorcycle

14. a. see the movie
    b. read the book

15. a. cocktail music
    b. disco music

16. a. do research in the library
    b. attend a classroom lecture

17. a. a hot drink
    b. a warm drink

18. a. a drum solo
    b. a string solo

19. a. too much exercise
    b. too little exercise

20. a. loud music
    b. quiet music

ANSWER SHEET

(Tear Out)

	A	B		A	B		A	B		A	B
1.	_____	_____	12.	_____	_____	23.	_____	_____	39.	_____	_____
2.	_____	_____	13.	_____	_____	24.	_____	_____	40.	_____	_____
3.	_____	_____	14.	_____	_____	25.	_____	_____	41.	_____	_____
4.	_____	_____	15.	_____	_____	26.	_____	_____	42.	_____	_____
5.	_____	_____	16.	_____	_____	27.	_____	_____	43.	_____	_____
6.	_____	_____	17.	_____	_____	28.	_____	_____	44.	_____	_____
7.	_____	_____	18.	_____	_____	29.	_____	_____	45.	_____	_____
8.	_____	_____	19.	_____	_____	30.	_____	_____	46.	_____	_____
9.	_____	_____	20.	_____	_____	31.	_____	_____	47.	_____	_____
10.	_____	_____	21.	_____	_____	32.	_____	_____	48.	_____	_____
11.	_____	_____	22.	_____	_____	33.	_____	_____	49.	_____	_____
						34.	_____	_____	50.	_____	_____
						35.	_____	_____	51.	_____	_____
						36.	_____	_____	52.	_____	_____
						37.	_____	_____	53.	_____	_____
						38.	_____	_____	54.	_____	_____

ANSWER SHEET

(Tear Out)

	A	B		A	B		A	B		A	B
1.	_____	_____	12.	_____	_____	23.	_____	_____	39.	_____	_____
2.	_____	_____	13.	_____	_____	24.	_____	_____	40.	_____	_____
3.	_____	_____	14.	_____	_____	25.	_____	_____	41.	_____	_____
4.	_____	_____	15.	_____	_____	26.	_____	_____	42.	_____	_____
5.	_____	_____	16.	_____	_____	27.	_____	_____	43.	_____	_____
6.	_____	_____	17.	_____	_____	28.	_____	_____	44.	_____	_____
7.	_____	_____	18.	_____	_____	29.	_____	_____	45.	_____	_____
8.	_____	_____	19.	_____	_____	30.	_____	_____	46.	_____	_____
9.	_____	_____	20.	_____	_____	31.	_____	_____	47.	_____	_____
10.	_____	_____	21.	_____	_____	32.	_____	_____	48.	_____	_____
11.	_____	_____	22.	_____	_____	33.	_____	_____	49.	_____	_____
						34.	_____	_____	50.	_____	_____
						35.	_____	_____	51.	_____	_____
						36.	_____	_____	52.	_____	_____
						37.	_____	_____	53.	_____	_____
						38.	_____	_____	54.	_____	_____

21. a. prepare medications
    b. dress wounds

22. a. a driving beat
    b. a nice melody

23. a. hard rock music
    b. regular popular music

24. a. like athletics
    b. dislike athletics

25. a. unamplified music
    b. electrically amplified music

26. a. smooth-textured foods
    b. crunchy foods

27. a. mind-expanding drugs
    b. alcohol

28. a. speed
    b. safety

29. a. the Beatles
    b. Dean Martin

30. a. soccer
    b. golf

31. a. excitement
    b. calm

32. a. a family of six
    b. a family of three

33. a. thrills
    b. tranquillity

34. a. play contact sports
    b. play noncontact sports

35. a. live in a crowded home
    b. live alone

36. a. share intimacy
    b. share affection

37. a. games emphasizing speed
    b. games paced slowly

38. a. thinking
    b. doing

39. a. competitive sports
    b. noncompetitive sports

40. a. emotionally expressive, somewhat
       unstable people
    b. calm, even-tempered people

41. a. be a nurse on an acute care ward
    b. be a nursing supervisor

42. a. be a NASA scientist
    b. be an astronaut

43. a. be a stuntman
    b. be a propman

44. a. a job which requires a lot of traveling
    b. a job which keeps you in one place

45. a. climb a mountain
    b. read about a dangerous adventure

46. a. body odors are disgusting
    b. body odors are appealing

47. a. keep on the move
    b. spend time relaxing

48. a. have a cold drink
    b. have a cool drink

49. a. being confined alone in a room
    b. being free in the desert

50. a. security
    b. excitement

51. a. continuous anesthesia
    b. continuous hallucinations

52. a. water skiing
    b. boat rowing

53. a. hostility
    b. conformity

54. a. Renoir
    b. Picasso

ANSWER KEY

1. a	12. b	23. a	39. a
2. a	13. b	24. a	40. a
3. a	14. a	25. b	41. a
4. a	15. b	26. b	42. b
5. a	16. b	27. a	43. a
6. a	17. a	28. a	44. a
7. b	18. a	29. a	45. a
8. b	19. a	30. a	46. b
9. a	20. a	31. a	47. a
10. b	21. b	32. a	48. a
11. a	22. a	33. a	49. b
		34. a	50. b
		35. a	51. b
		36. b	52. a
		37. a	53. a
		38. b	54. b

SCORING THE SCALE

Compare your answers on the answer sheet to the answer Key above. Give yourself one point for each matching answer and write the total in the box below.

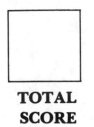

**TOTAL
SCORE**

INTERPRETING YOUR SCORE

Low Scorers (0–15)—People who score low on this scale generally like to play it safe. As a low scorer, you are expressing a preference for low levels of stimulation and a quiet life-style, probably by yourself or with very few other people. You are not likely to be involved with heavy smoking or anything else that could pose a risk for you. As someone perhaps overly sensitive to sensory stimulation, however, you probably find yourself worrying about many physical problems. Much of your concern may be the *anticipation* of more severe problems since you tend to react to lower levels of stimulation and pain than most people.

Average Scorers (16–39)—Average scorers are in the range which relates to a normal flexibility in handling sensory stimulation and pain. Scores here reflect a mixture of desire for excitement in some things and for tranquillity in others. Since the concepts of reducer and augmenter relate to several areas of stimulation—social, physical, cognitive—a review of your answers may show an interesting preference for high or low activity in one or two of these areas.

High Scorers (40–54)—High scorers can generally be described as people hungry for stimulation. They tend to be extroverted, high-energy people who may be seen by others as always out for excitement, even at the risk of great pain. If you are a high scorer, you probably prefer speed over safety, excitement over security, and thrills to tranquillity. On the positive side, high scorers are not afraid of health problems and show few somatic complaints. But they also tend to be heavy smokers, both for the stimulation smoking offers and the lack of fear of potential illness. The dangers in being such an action-oriented individual range from the high possibility of a serious accident to exhaustion—the body can go at top speed for only so long. If this is true for you, you might want to slow down enough to thoroughly examine the risks.

ABOUT THE SCALE

Algophobia—the fear of pain—prevents many people from achieving the enjoyment out of life they would like. Being unable to tolerate pain on any level forces people into lives devoid of excitement and risk. Rather than travel, engage in competitive sports, or even golf, for example, extremely low pain-tolerant individuals may be too frightened to do much except sit at home. Such people value safety, even at the expense of fun and stimulation, because of their fear of possible pain.

Research by Dr. Asenath Petrie during the 1950s and 1960s examined the relationship between pain tolerance and the functioning of the prefrontal cortex part of the brain. She used the terms "reducer" and "augmenter" to describe people who were high- and low-pain-tolerant respectively. Dr. Petrie found that people who could accept high levels of pain tended to underestimate (reduce) the size of a task, while low-pain-tolerant individuals overestimated (augmented) the task.

Her work was followed in 1969 by that of psychologist Alan Vando. Dr. Vando wrote,

. . . the manner in which a person processes pain perceptually, as reflected in his pain tolerance, is related to a more general phenomenon of how he processes stimulation in all sensory modalities.

He then developed the Reducer-Augmenter Scale to measure these hypothesized differences in how people react to pain and other types of stimulation. Since his aim was to test for a desire or liking for stimulation, he designed his scale to force people to choose between two situations of contrasting stimulus intensity. Thus someone who is high in pain tolerance, a reducer, would choose situations which involve high stimulation and avoid low ones, while the augmenter would select the opposite situations. His scale has proven to be a useful measure in a variety of research situations. One particularly interesting project used his scale to help in bioastronaut crew selection prior to their three-man, 105-day isolation periods. Other studies, as you will see discussed in the scale interpretation, have examined pain tolerance in relation to extroversion, physical complaints, and even smoking.

CHAPTER FIVE

Marital & Family Relationships

*E*very emotion from the tenderest love to violent rage can be found in that oft-tangled web of relations between husband and wife, child and parent, brother and sister. While psychologists have long studied family relations with regard to the development of neurosis, other social scientists have begun to study the family because of the appalling rise in violent behavior in our society. When the problem of social violence was first examined, it was found that a disproportionate amount of the violence occurs between members of the same family.

If there is a considerable amount of tension and conflict in your family, but you are able to live with it day by day, you are probably doing better than the average family. A quick look at the statistics makes one wonder whether *any* family lives in peace. Divorce is epidemic, battered wives and abused children number in the tens and hundreds of thousands, sexual therapy and marriage, family, and child counseling are booming professions.

The members of such an interdependent, socially enmeshed group—the family—cannot help but have some problems understanding one another's behavior. Because they are so close, people in family situations often fail to perceive some dimensions of their own behavior. Marital, parental, sexual, and sibling relations are each complex and often troublesome worlds by themselves. When you put all these delicate equations together in the same physical space, then increase internal pressures by forcing them to cope with the demands of today's external world, you have a formula for certain conflict. Since conflict is unavoidable by the very nature of the family structure, the answer lies in understanding and managing the conflict as it occurs, to keep it from getting out of hand.

In cases of severe family conflict, the collective blind spots of the family members make it necessary to call in outside help in the form of a counselor, an arbiter, or a therapist. When these outside interventions are effective, as they often can be, it is almost always because the intervening agent has found a way to show the family what it is doing. Just as self-knowledge is at the root of all individual psychotherapy, some means of objective self-observation is basic to all types of family therapy. Psychodrama, videotape, and other techniques are used, but testing is still one of the psychologists' most powerful tools in understanding family situations. Much can be learned about the component dimensions of family behavior by isolating stresses, conflicts, and rivalries within a particular family. Strong points such as loyalties, stabilizing factors, and common goals are also uncovered by such tests. Taken together, the awareness of these strengths and weaknesses can lead to much improved family relations.

Marital Adjustment Test

by Harvey J. Locke and Karl M. Wallace

On the test below are 15 questions. Read each one and determine the number of points that best describe your relationship with your mate. Write that number in the answer column on the right.

---

1. Find the point on the scale line below which best describes the degree of happiness, everything considered, of your present marriage. The middle point, "happy," represents the degree of happiness which most people get from marriage, and the scale gradually ranges on one side to those few who are very unhappy in marriage, and on the other to those few who experience extreme joy or felicity in marriage. Write the number of points in the answer column.

0	2	7	15	20	25	35

| Very Unhappy | | Happy | | | | Perfectly Happy | ☐ 1 |

To what extent do you and your mate agree on the following items? Note the points in the answer column.

	Always Agree	Almost Always Agree	Occasionally Disagree	Frequently Disagree	Almost Always Disagree	Always Disagree	
2. Handling family finances	5	4	3	2	1	0	☐ 2
3. Matters of recreation	5	4	3	2	1	0	☐ 3
4. Demonstrations of affection	8	6	4	2	1	0	☐ 4
5. Friends	5	4	3	2	1	0	☐ 5
6. Sex relations	15	12	9	4	1	0	☐ 6
7. Conventionality (right, good, or proper conduct)	5	4	3	2	1	0	☐ 7
8. Philosophy of life	5	4	3	2	1	0	☐ 8
9. Ways of dealing with in-laws	5	4	3	2	1	0	☐ 9

10. When disagreements arise, they usually result in: husband giving in (0), wife giving in (2), agreement by mutual give and take (10). ☐ 10

11. Do you and your mate engage in outside interests together: All of them (10), some of them (8), very few of them (3), none of them (0)? ☐ 11

12. In leisure time, do you generally prefer: to be "on the go" _____, to stay at home _____? Does your mate generally prefer to be "on the go" _____, to stay at home_____? (Stay at home for both, 16 points; "on the go" for both, 3 points; disagreement, 2 points.) ☐ 12

13. Do you ever wish you had not married? Frequently (0), occasionally (3), rarely (8), never (15). ☐ 13

14. If you had your life to live over, do you think you would marry the same person (15), marry a different person (0), not marry at all (1)? ☐ 14

15. Do you confide in your mate: almost never (0), rarely (2), in most things (10), in everything (10)? ☐ 15

SCORING THE TEST

To find your score add up the points that you recorded next to the questions. This total is your score.

INTERPRETING YOUR SCORE

Low Scorers (2–99)—Scores in the lower end of this range (2–75) suggest serious to severe problems in the marital relationship; the lower the score, the greater the reported dissatisfaction. Scores in the upper range (76–99) indicate moderate but probably manageable marital difficulties. If you scored here, you probably did not need this test to tell you of your unhappiness, but it can still serve to indicate which areas seem to be your biggest concerns. Taking some of the other tests in this chapter can also help you gain a clearer understanding of what might be at the core of your dissatisfaction. Of course, such an examination is only a first step—though an extremely important one. After this you must focus on what to do about the problems. These tests can, hopefully, serve to stimulate discussion between the two of you; you may find that you both share the same concerns and that the relationship possesses more mutual support than you realized. If so, more serious problems can be avoided through an exchange of ideas and an understanding of each other's attitudes and feelings. This may be difficult for you without outside professional help since old habits are hard to break and communication can be hard to initiate. But such help can bring out the best in both of you as individuals and draw on the potential that is present in your relationship.

High Scorers (100–158)—In the original study by Drs. Locke and Wallace, 96 percent of their well-adjusted couples scored 100 or higher. So if you scored here, you are in satisfied company. Of course, you and your spouse may find an occasional area or two for a few rounds of sparring, but the relationship is most likely a mutually positive one. Additional research has shown that couples with high marital adjustment scores usually are made up of two people with high individual self-esteem. Such marriages may be successful, as one psychologist wrote, "because they are two self-accepting, competent people who also happen to be husbands or wives."

ABOUT THE TEST

The increasing incidence of divorce over the last several years points up the need for couples to examine their marital relationship before the problems get beyond their control. The usual pattern for dissatisfied couples is that both seem reluctant to objectively examine the problems they are having. Such problems then linger and often increase in importance until divorce appears to be the only alternative to "incompatibility."

Such a process does not have to be the inevitable one for distressed couples to follow. Early examination of needs that are not being met, issues that are unclear, and common goals for the future can prevent more serious, debilitating problems from arising. The primary approach of marital therapy involves exactly that examination.

Thus methods for assessing marital satisfaction are extremely important in the development and evaluation of treatment programs with dissatisfied couples. Such tests facilitate the identification of marital problems, giving the couple focal points for discussion. One of the marital inventories, which has served as a model for many others, is the Marital Adjustment Test by Dr. Harvey Locke and Dr. Karl Wallace. Prior to their work, most marital satisfaction tests were too long and complex for easy use in the marital therapy situation. The goal of Drs. Locke and Wallace was to produce a test which contained "only the most basic or fundamental items." The fact that their test is very frequently used today in research and clinical treatment speaks for its effectiveness.

Index of Family Relations

by Walter W. Hudson

This questionnaire is designed to measure the way you feel about your family as a whole. It is not a test so there are no right or wrong answers. Answer each item as carefully and accurately as you can by placing a number beside each one as follows:

1 = *Rarely or none of the time*

2 = *A little of the time*

3 = *Some of the time*

4 = *A good part of the time*

5 = *Most or all of the time*

1. The members of my family really care about each other. _____ 1.
2. I think my family is terrific. _____ 2.
3. My family gets on my nerves. _____ 3.
4. I really enjoy my family. _____ 4.
5. I can really depend on my family. _____ 5.
6. I really do not care to be around my family. _____ 6.
7. I wish I was not part of this family. _____ 7.
8. I get along well with my family. _____ 8.
9. Members of my family argue too much. _____ 9.
10. There is no sense of closeness in my family. _____ 10.
11. I feel like a stranger in my family. _____ 11.
12. My family does not understand me. _____ 12.
13. There is too much hatred in my family. _____ 13.
14. Members of my family are really good to one another. _____ 14.
15. My family is well respected by those who know us. _____ 15.
16. There seems to be a lot of friction in my family. _____ 16.
17. There is a lot of love in my family. _____ 17.
18. Members of my family get along well together. _____ 18.
19. Life in my family is generally unpleasant. _____ 19.
20. My family is a great joy to me. _____ 20.
21. I feel proud of my family. _____ 21.
22. Other families seem to get along better than ours. _____ 22.
23. My family is a real source of comfort to me. _____ 23.
24. I feel left out of my family. _____ 24.
25. My family is an unhappy one. _____ 25.

INTERPRETING YOUR SCORE

Low Scorers (0–29)—Low scorers are reporting a high level of family satisfaction. If you scored here, you are saying that, in general, you are happy to be a member of your family, and that your family serves as a source of happiness for you. When your own individual day-to-day concerns build, you can probably turn to one or more of your family for comfort and support over your own rough periods. Though, as in any social relationship, your family has its difficulties, the members of your family get along well together and exhibit collective as well as individual high self-esteem.

High Scorers (30–100)—The higher your score on this index, the more dissatisfaction with your family you are reporting. Of course, scores between 30 and 40 must be interpreted with caution. Momentary stresses may be present in your family which make things seem more unpleasant now than they usually are. But if you scored much higher than 40 or feel that your score does reflect the general state of your family life, you are in need of some serious reflection about the way your family works and lives together. It is likely that such family unhappiness has made its way into the individual lives of each family member. In addition, members have likely lost a source of support which is often needed as personal stresses increase. Perhaps this knowledge can lead to some open discussions among your family members and a renewal of the warmth that was once there. If your family problems make such communication difficult, however, professional counseling can help rebuild those bridges to one another.

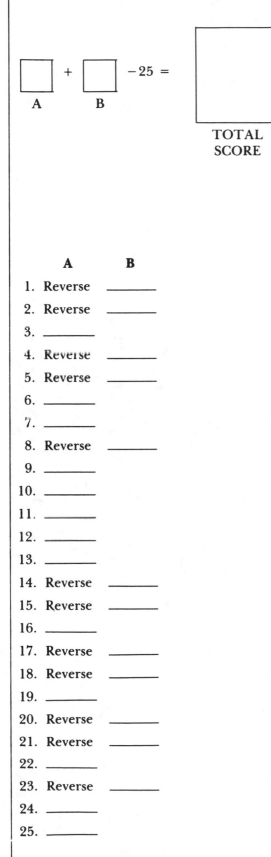

SCORING KEY

A + B − 25 =

TOTAL
SCORE

	A	B
1.	Reverse	___
2.	Reverse	___
3.	___	
4.	Reverse	___
5.	Reverse	___
6.	___	
7.	___	
8.	Reverse	___
9.	___	
10.	___	
11.	___	
12.	___	
13.	___	
14.	Reverse	___
15.	Reverse	___
16.	___	
17.	Reverse	___
18.	Reverse	___
19.	___	
20.	Reverse	___
21.	Reverse	___
22.	___	
23.	Reverse	___
24.	___	
25.	___	

SCORING THE INDEX

Fold the facing page forward along the dotted line to compare your answers with the Scoring Key.

First, transfer your answers into the spaces in Column A for items 3, 6, 7, 9, etc.

Next, in Column B, reverse the numerical value of your answers for items 1, 2, 4, 5, etc. For example:

In Column B, an answer of

1 earns 5 points

2 earns 4 points

3 earns 3 points

4 earns 2 points

5 earns 1 point

To find your final score add together the total points in Column A and the total points in Column B. From this sum *subtract* 25 points. The result is your final score.

ABOUT THE INDEX

The English poet John Donne wrote, "No man is an island, entire of itself; every man is a piece of the continent, a part of the main." For many of us, that continent is our family, those people with whom we share ourselves each day. The family can be a source of great positive energy, encouraging us to try new things and supporting us when our attempts fall short. But for some, the family situation is a source of stress and frustration, pulling energy away from us rather than feeding our needs. These needs that are not met belong to *all* the family members, for no one is immune to the effects of a stressful family life. Children may show it through physical complaints or school problems, while mom and dad may show the pressure in marital conflicts or behaviors which remove them from family contact, such as drinking or an endless list of things to do away from home. Both the individual family members and their intertwined relationships rise or fall on the health of the family unit.

For more than thirty years, family researchers have been concerned with the evaluation of the family process. As with any other complex process, attempts have been made to specify what it is in family relationships that can cause problems. Some of the other tests in this chapter are the results of that work, such as marital roles and sexual compatibility, but Dr. Walter Hudson saw the need for a global measure of family satisfaction—an index that went directly to the question, "How do you feel about being a member of this family?" In 1977, he developed the Index of Family Relations as part of his series of tests for use in psychological and social work treatment. We have included it here because of its straightforward way of evaluating family satisfaction.

Marital Role Decisions Questionnaire

by Joseph E. Grush and Janet G. Yehl

Beginning below you will find a number of situations described in which married couples had to make difficult decisions. After you have carefully read each situation, pick one of the two alternative courses of action with which you most agree. Then indicate your degree of agreement by choosing the "strongly agree," "moderately agree," or "slightly agree" categories. For each situation, choose only one alternative and place only one check mark on the answer sheet. If you truly cannot decide, check the statement, "I honestly cannot decide between these two alternatives." Tear out the answer sheet on the next page to record your answers. A duplicate of the answer sheet is printed on the back.

1. Bob and Helen are both twenty-four. Bob has just completed graduate school. He has been hired by a good company at a substantial salary. Bob and Helen would like to start a family immediately. Alternatively, delaying their family for three years would allow Helen to return to college and complete her degree.

Bob and Helen should begin their family immediately.
   A. strongly agree
   B. moderately agree
   C. slightly agree

Bob and Helen should wait to start their family until Helen finishes college.
   D. strongly agree
   E. moderately agree
   F. slightly agree
   G. I honestly cannot decide between these two alternatives.

2. Tom and Sue have been invited to attend the wedding ceremony and reception of Tom's longtime friend who is not very well known to Sue. Sue's close friends have planned to get together on the same day and time as the wedding of Tom's friends. Sue's friends have invited Sue to attend.

Tom and Sue should go to the wedding together.
   A. strongly agree
   B. moderately agree
   C. slightly agree

Tom should go to the wedding and Sue should go to her friends' get-together.
   D. strongly agree
   E. moderately agree
   F. slightly agree
   G. I honestly cannot decide between these two alternatives.

3. Karen and Jack were recently married. Shortly after their honeymoon, one of their acquaintances talked to them about life insurance. It turned out that both Karen and Jack already have insurance policies which would cover their burial expenses. The acquaintance suggested that they should consider buying additional life insurance. Karen and Jack decide that they can afford to buy an additional $20,000 worth of life insurance.

Karen and Jack should buy a $10,000 policy on Karen's life and $10,000 on Jack's life.
   A. strongly agree
   B. moderately agree
   C. slightly agree

Karen and Jack should buy a $20,000 policy on Jack's life.

- D. strongly agree
- E. moderately agree
- F. slightly agree
- G. I honestly cannot decide between these two alternatives.

4. Peter and Joann were recently married. Peter is a third-year graduate student and Joann is working. Shortly after they moved into their first apartment, Peter and Joann were discussing various topics related to their new married state. Peter said that he would like to help with the household chores, but if he did this he would be taking valuable time away from his studies. Since Peter was in a highly competitive field where jobs were becoming scarce, he felt that Joann should handle the household chores so he could devote more time to his studies and enhance his prospects for obtaining a good job.

Peter should help Joann with the household chores.

- A. strongly agree
- B. moderately agree
- C. slightly agree

Peter should devote his time to his studies.

- D. strongly agree
- E. moderately agree
- F. slightly agree
- G. I honestly cannot decide between these two alternatives.

5. Mike and Sally are both teachers. They have two children, ages nine and seven. Assuming that both Mike and Sally could get off from work, who should stay home with the children when they are sick on a school day?

Sally and Mike should take turns staying home with the children.

- A. strongly agree
- B. moderately agree
- C. slightly agree

Sally should stay home with the children.

- D. strongly agree
- E. moderately agree
- F. slightly agree
- G. I honestly cannot decide between these two alternatives.

6. Barb and Ed are going to be married soon. Barb wants to keep her maiden name as her legal name after marriage. Ed is ambivalent about Barb's keeping her maiden name. Aside from his own feelings, Ed is concerned about the feelings of his parents, who are confused and disturbed by Barb's intention to keep her maiden name.

Barb should take Ed's last name as her legal name.

- A. strongly agree
- B. moderately agree
- C. slightly agree

Barb should keep her maiden name as her legal name.

- D. strongly agree
- E. moderately agree
- F. slightly agree
- G. I honestly cannot decide between these two alternatives.

7. John and Therese are married with children in primary school. John's company has just offered him a promotion and a large raise. Accepting the promotion means that John would move up the corporate ladder in salary and responsibility. Accepting the promotion also means that John and Therese would have to move to another city which is 750 miles away from their families, friends, and a part-time job that Therese enjoys. John's company made it clear that turning down his promotion and transfer would not jeopardize his present job or future opportunities with the company.

John and Therese should accept the promotion and transfer.

- A. strongly agree
- B. moderately agree
- C. slightly agree

John and Therese should turn down the promotion and transfer.

- D. strongly agree
- E. moderately agree
- F. slightly agree
- G. I honestly cannot decide between these two alternatives.

8. Mary Ann and Dick have a two-year-old son. Although Mary Ann and Dick do not need the money, Mary Ann would like to work full time at a job that she was just offered. Accepting the job would require putting their child in a day nursery.

Mary Ann and Dick should place the child in a day nursery so Mary Ann can work.

- A. strongly agree
- B. moderately agree
- C. slightly agree

ANSWER SHEET
(Tear Out)

Check only one answer per item.

1. _____ A	2. _____ A	3. _____ A	4. _____ A
_____ B	_____ B	_____ B	_____ B
_____ C	_____ C	_____ C	_____ C
_____ D	_____ D	_____ D	_____ D
_____ E	_____ E	_____ E	_____ E
_____ F	_____ F	_____ F	_____ F
_____ G	_____ G	_____ G	_____ G

5. _____ A	6. _____ A	7. _____ A	8. _____ A
_____ B	_____ B	_____ B	_____ B
_____ C	_____ C	_____ C	_____ C
_____ D	_____ D	_____ D	_____ D
_____ E	_____ E	_____ E	_____ E
_____ F	_____ F	_____ F	_____ F
_____ G	_____ G	_____ G	_____ G

9. _____ A	10. _____ A	11. _____ A	12. _____ A
_____ B	_____ B	_____ B	_____ B
_____ C	_____ C	_____ C	_____ C
_____ D	_____ D	_____ D	_____ D
_____ E	_____ E	_____ E	_____ E
_____ F	_____ F	_____ F	_____ F
_____ G	_____ G	_____ G	_____ G

ANSWER SHEET
(Tear Out)

Check only one answer per item.

1. _____ A	2. _____ A	3. _____ A	4. _____ A
_____ B	_____ B	_____ B	_____ B
_____ C	_____ C	_____ C	_____ C
_____ D	_____ D	_____ D	_____ D
_____ E	_____ E	_____ E	_____ E
_____ F	_____ F	_____ F	_____ F
_____ G	_____ G	_____ G	_____ G
5. _____ A	6. _____ A	7. _____ A	8. _____ A
_____ B	_____ B	_____ B	_____ B
_____ C	_____ C	_____ C	_____ C
_____ D	_____ D	_____ D	_____ D
_____ E	_____ E	_____ E	_____ E
_____ F	_____ F	_____ F	_____ F
_____ G	_____ G	_____ G	_____ G
9. _____ A	10. _____ A	11. _____ A	12. _____ A
_____ B	_____ B	_____ B	_____ B
_____ C	_____ C	_____ C	_____ C
_____ D	_____ D	_____ D	_____ D
_____ E	_____ E	_____ E	_____ E
_____ F	_____ F	_____ F	_____ F
_____ G	_____ G	_____ G	_____ G

Mary Ann and Dick should not place the child in a day nursery.
- D. strongly agree
- E. moderately agree
- F. slightly agree
- G. I honestly cannot decide between these two alternatives.

9. Helen and Nick are preparing themselves to become social workers. Helen's parents have an established family business. They want Helen and Nick to join the family business immediately so that they can learn the business and be ready to take over when her folks retire in a few years. Neither Helen nor Nick is really interested in the family business, but it would definitely offer them financial security. Both Helen and Nick really enjoy social work, but the job market is becoming increasingly tight and their financial security would definitely be less certain.

Helen and Nick should join the family business.
- A. strongly agree
- B. moderately agree
- C. slightly agree

Helen and Nick should pursue careers in social work.
- D. strongly agree
- E. moderately agree
- F. slightly agree
- G. I honestly cannot decide between these two alternatives.

10. Phyllis and Eric have just completed their advanced degrees. Eric has a job offer as an assistant professor at a prestigious university in a location where Phyllis would be unable to get a job in her field. Phyllis has a job offer in her field in a different city where Eric has an offer to teach at a junior college.

Eric and Phyllis should accept the university position.
- A. strongly agree
- B. moderately agree
- C. slightly agree

Eric and Phyllis should accept positions in the city where they both could work.
- D. strongly agree
- E. moderately agree
- F. slightly agree
- G. I honestly cannot decide between these two alternatives.

11. Bill is a high school principal and Amy teaches at a community college. The night that Bill's school has its annual athletic banquet is the same night that Amy's school has scheduled its staff party. Bill must attend the athletic banquet to present awards and to deliver a speech. Amy has always enjoyed her school's staff parties in the past.

Amy should go to her school's staff party.
- A. strongly agree
- B. moderately agree
- C. slightly agree

Amy should go with Bill to his school's athletic banquet.
- D. strongly agree
- E. moderately agree
- F. slightly agree
- G. I honestly cannot decide between these two alternatives.

12. Joan and Harry have just learned that Joan is two months pregnant with their first child. Hearing the news, they decide to discuss their housing situation. They are currently renting a comfortable three-bedroom apartment. Financially, they can afford to make a down payment on their own home. Continuing to rent has the advantage of greater flexibility and mobility. Buying has the advantage of owning their own home. When taxes, insurance, and mortgage payments are considered, buying a home has no financial advantage over renting.

Harry and Joan should continue to rent the apartment.
- A. strongly agree
- B. moderately agree
- C. slightly agree

Harry and Joan should buy their own home.
- D. strongly agree
- E. moderately agree
- F. slightly agree
- G. I honestly cannot decide between these two alternatives.

SCORING KEY

1.	A	7
	B	6
	C	5
	D	1
	E	2
	F	3
	G	4

2.	A	7
	B	6
	C	5
	D	1
	E	2
	F	3
	G	4

3.	A	1
	B	2
	C	3
	D	7
	E	6
	F	5
	G	4

4.	A	1
	B	2
	C	3
	D	7
	E	6
	F	5
	G	4

5.	A	1
	B	2
	C	3
	D	7
	E	6
	F	5
	G	4

6.	A	7
	B	6
	C	5
	D	1
	E	2
	F	3
	G	4

7.	A	7
	B	6
	C	5
	D	1
	E	2
	F	3
	G	4

8.	A	1
	B	2
	C	3
	D	7
	E	6
	F	5
	G	4

9.	A	7
	B	6
	C	5
	D	1
	E	2
	F	3
	G	4

10.	A	7
	B	6
	C	5
	D	1
	E	2
	F	3
	G	4

11.	A	1
	B	2
	C	3
	D	7
	E	6
	F	5
	G	4

12.	A	1
	B	2
	C	3
	D	7
	E	6
	F	5
	G	4

SCORING THE QUESTIONNAIRE

To find your score, compare your answer sheet to the Scoring Key on the facing page. Find the number of points that is indicated by your answer and write that number on your answer sheet. Add up all your points and write that number in the box below.

TOTAL SCORE

INTERPRETING YOUR SCORE

Low Scorers (12–30)—As a low scorer, you are answering in a nontraditional direction. Your responses stress the equality of men and women as marriage partners and state that the husband and wife should function as individuals as well as a marital unit. For comparison, consider that Drs. Grush and Yehl found that a sample of members from NOW (National Organization for Women) averaged a score of 21 on this scale. As a person with a nontraditional view of the marital decision-making process, it could be important for you to be certain that your partner both knows your strong feelings and also shares at least some of them. The second copy of the answer sheet given to your partner could provide you both with some interesting points for the discussion.

Average Scorers (31–50)—Average scorers could be answering in a middle-of-the-road fashion or be mixing extreme traditional and nontraditional views depending on the issue involved. If you achieved your average score through the first method, answering three, four, or five for most of the questions, your score could reflect a flexibility in thinking about the roles of men and women in marriage. This suggests that you are open to examining those roles and could be compatible with a spouse holding traditional or nontraditional views. If you obtained your average score through a combination of ones and sevens, however, you are reporting a mix of extreme traditional and nontraditional views. Look back over the situations in the questionnaire in light of the five areas of concern discussed in the "About This Questionnaire" section on the next page. It is important for you and your marriage partner to know where your extreme views match (or don't match) across those issues.

High Scorers (51–84)—High scorers are emphasizing the traditional marital roles of men and women on the questionnaire. These roles stress the man as the breadwinner and primary focus for career decisions, while the woman is primarily supportive in her roles as mother and housewife. In the study by Drs. Grush and Yehl, a group of policemen averaged 57 on the questionnaire, while their wives averaged 51. Such compatibility speaks well for overall marital satisfaction if the couple's scores match across specific areas. Major differences in an area or two, however, could lead to problems in the marriage if such differences are not examined and worked out.

ABOUT THE QUESTIONNAIRE

Although opposites may attract, psychological research has established the fact that a similarity in attitudes and ideas creates the strongest interpersonal attraction. We may initially be drawn to someone who thinks and acts quite differently from the way we do, but it is hard to build a lasting relationship on disagreement. The stresses in marriage go beyond decisions about where to go for dinner or what movie to see. Extreme differences of opinions on issues such as children, finances, and careers place a potentially destructive strain on the relationship and on the emotional stability of the people involved. Husband and wife roles in the family are central to many other potential conflicts. As more families have two wage earners, the views of both husband and wife toward the marital decision process become significant. An increasing number of men and women are asking for equality in deciding how the money is spent, who takes care of the children, and whose career is emphasized.

As part of a research program examining the impact of roles and disposition on interpersonal attraction, psychologists Joseph Grush and Janet Yehl developed the Marital Role Decisions Questionnaire. The questionnaire was needed for the selection of individuals who had traditional or nontraditional orientations toward sex roles and marriage. Drs. Grush and Yehl obtained possible items for their questionnaire by asking twenty married couples to respond to open-ended questions that asked them to describe:

(a) important decisions that you and your spouse (or couples you know) had to make where the two of you had opposing viewpoints, and (b) the choices that were available to you and your spouse (or couples you know).

The twelve situations retained for the questionnaire covered five areas of concern: domestic, financial, social, familial, and career, allowing the person taking the test to choose from traditional or nontraditional ways of resolving the conflict.

Index of Sexual Satisfaction

by Walter W. Hudson

This questionnaire is designed to measure the degree of satisfaction you have in the sexual relationship with your partner. It is not a test, so there are no right or wrong answers. Answer each item as carefully and accurately as you can by placing a number beside each one as follows:

1 = Rarely or none of the time

2 = A little of the time

3 = Sometime

4 = Good part of the time

5 = Most or all of the time

_____ 1. I feel that my partner enjoys our sex life.

_____ 2. My sex life is very exciting.

_____ 3. Sex is fun for my partner and me.

_____ 4. I feel that my partner sees little in me except for the sex I can give.

_____ 5. I feel that sex is dirty and disgusting.

_____ 6. My sex life is monotonous.

_____ 7. When we have sex it is too rushed and hurriedly completed.

_____ 8. I feel that my sex life is lacking quality.

_____ 9. My partner is sexually very exciting.

_____ 10. I enjoy the sex techniques that my partner likes or uses.

_____ 11. I feel that my partner wants too much sex from me.

_____ 12. I think that sex is wonderful.

_____ 13. My partner dwells on sex too much.

_____ 14. I feel that sex is something that has to be endured in our relationship.

_____ 15. My partner is too rough or brutal when we have sex.

_____ 16. My partner observes good personal hygiene.

_____ 17. I feel that sex is a normal function of our relationship.

_____ 18. My partner does not want sex when I do.

_____ 19. I feel that our sex life really adds a lot to our relationship.

_____ 20. I would like to have sexual contact with someone other than my partner.

_____ 21. It is easy for me to get sexually excited by my partner.

_____ 22. I feel that my partner is sexually pleased with me.

_____ 23. My partner is very sensitive to my sexual needs and desires.

_____ 24. I feel that I should have sex more often.

_____ 25. I feel that my sex life is boring.

SCORING KEY

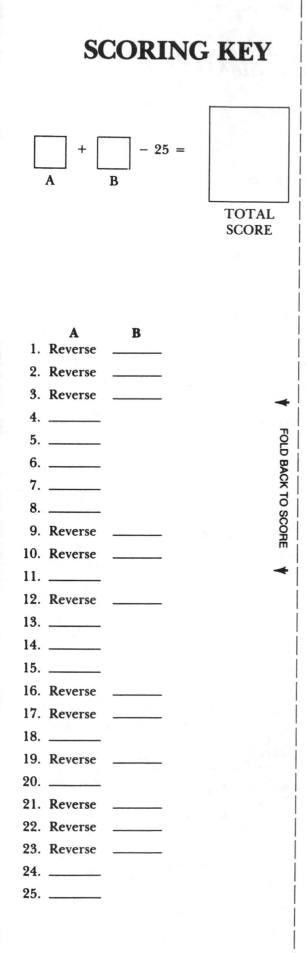

$\boxed{}$ + $\boxed{}$ − 25 = $\boxed{}$

A   B   TOTAL
SCORE

      A   **B**

1. Reverse _____
2. Reverse _____
3. Reverse _____
4. _____
5. _____
6. _____
7. _____
8. _____
9. Reverse _____
10. Reverse _____
11. _____
12. Reverse _____
13. _____
14. _____
15. _____
16. Reverse _____
17. Reverse _____
18. _____
19. Reverse _____
20. _____
21. Reverse _____
22. Reverse _____
23. Reverse _____
24. _____
25. _____

FOLD BACK TO SCORE

SCORING THE INDEX

To score the index, fold this page back along the dotted line to line up your answers with the Scoring Key.

First, transfer your answers into the spaces in Column A for items 4, 5, 6, 7, etc.

Next, in Column B, reverse the numerical value of your answers for items 1, 2, 3, 9, etc. For example:

In Column B, an answer of

1 earns 5 points
2 earns 4 points
3 earns 3 points
4 earns 2 points
5 earns 1 point

To find your final score, add together the total points in Column A and the total points in Column B. From this sum, subtract 25 points. The result is your final score.

INTERPRETING YOUR SCORE

Low Scorers (0–29)—As a low scorer on this index, you are reporting little dissatisfaction with your sex life as it is. You and your partner apparently have worked out a mutually enjoyable and stimulating balance to your sexual experiences. Particularly for younger adults, such sexual satisfaction is often associated with good feelings about themselves and life in general. For low scorers of any age, sexual compatibility suggests the likelihood that their present relationship is a lasting one, and that they are able to work out disagreements in other areas as they appear.

High Scorers (30–100)—People who score in this range are expressing some level of dissatisfaction with their sexual relationship. Natu-rally, the higher the score the greater the dissatisfaction. High scorers tend to report associated dissatisfaction and discord in other areas of the marital relationship as well. If you are a young adult and have scored here, it is likely that such sexual unhappiness has also affected your levels of self-esteem and general good feelings about life. Research suggests that younger adults place much more emphasis upon sexual performance and gratification than do older people. In either case, scores in the higher levels of this range strongly suggest the need for professional assistance, either individual counseling for your own benefit or marital/couple counseling to work out problems in the relationship.

ABOUT THE INDEX

The well-known sex research team of Masters and Johnson estimate that over half the couples who seek divorce are having sexual problems. Even where divorce is not an immediate consideration, couples with problems often treat sex as a taboo subject, even though their sexual problems are creating a tremendous strain on their relationship. Fortunately the discussion of sex is becoming increasingly open as a social topic and psychological and medical treatment techniques have reached high levels of effectiveness. Dr. Walter Hudson points out, however, "The development of assessment devices for measuring sexual problems has largely been ignored, although the use of new treatment methods and the expansion of research in human sexuality increases the need for reliable and valid measurement tools in this area."

For many years, professionals such as medical doctors, psychologists, and social workers overlooked sexual satisfaction as a crucial part of marital satisfaction. Even where researchers attempted to build an inventory of sexual concerns, they have done it in a roundabout way, asking questions about marital roles and inferring sexual compatibility.

Dr. Hudson's goal was to provide the sex therapist with a measure of sexual satisfaction that had a clear focus on behaviors, attitudes, and affective responses to human sexuality. "Most important," he wrote, "counselors and researchers need a measurement device that will assist them to evaluate the quality of the sexual relationship between partners." He developed the Index of Sexual Satisfaction to meet this need.

CHAPTER SIX

Depression

*I*f you occasionally feel "blue," "down in the dumps," discouraged, dejected, despondent, or apathetic, it's a small comfort, at least, to know that you do not suffer alone: In a recent public poll, over *half* the people interviewed said that they were depressed much or some of the time. Up to 70 percent of college freshmen have reported feelings of depression, and 7 to 15 percent of the population suffers from moderate to severe depression at any one time. Cycles of elation and depression must be expected in a society that offers such a wide variety of things to be depressed about. Society, however, keeps functioning because most of us are able to pick ourselves up and do our jobs, even though we may not feel like it.

For most people most of the time, depression is an unpleasant emotion that goes away of its own accord—or after a hot bath, a long run, or a nap. For a minority of millions, however, depression can take on a life of its own. Depression is a major component in many neuroses and psychoses, and it can lead to thoughts and actions related to suicide. Prolonged, severe depression is a serious symptom that calls for immediate medical and psychological care, but mild to moderate depression is an unavoidable part of daily life.

Because of depression's role in emotional disorders, depression and its treatment have been thoroughly studied by psychologists. Theories about the causes and mechanisms of depression are as varied as theories of personality. The psychoanalytic school sees the roots of depression in very early childhood: According to Freud, you could not express anger toward your mother because you relied on her for so much. When she wasn't able to gratify your needs instantly, you felt strong displeasure. Instead of expressing anger, you turned the emotion on yourself and became depressed.

Cognitive psychologists view depression in terms of the ways people think about themselves, their world, and their future: if you distort experience so that your problems are magnified and your disappointments are exaggerated, you essentially talk yourself into being depressed. Behavioral psychologists take yet another point of view. They see depression as the direct result of a drop in the individual's level of everyday rewards. We all require a daily dose of essential "reinforcing stimuli" such as food, water, warmth, comfort, affection, and stimulation. When we are deprived of these reinforcers, we start acting depressed. When the depression affects our ability to go out and get the reinforcement we need, it becomes a downward spiral.

Some tests go right to the heart of the matter and attempt to measure feelings of depression. Other tests look at related dimensions of personality, such as self-esteem, contentment, and interests. Depression is not a pleasant part of the self to confront directly, but as we look at our own depressive tendencies, through both direct and indirect questions, we learn a great deal about the way we see ourselves and our world.

Beck Depression Inventory

by Aaron T. Beck

Read over the statements grouped with each letter, A through U. Pick out the statement within each group that best describes the way you feel today, that is, right at this moment. Circle the number next to the statement that you have chosen in each group. If two or more statements in a group describe the way you feel equally well, circle each one. Be sure to read over all of the statements in each group before you decide on one.

A. (Sadness)
    0 I do not feel sad.
    1 I feel blue or sad.
    2a I am blue or sad all the time and I can't snap out of it.
    2b I am so sad or unhappy that it is quite painful.
    3 I am so sad or unhappy that I can't stand it.

B. (Pessimism)
    0 I am not particularly pessimistic or discouraged about the future.
    1 I feel discouraged about the future.
    2a I feel I have nothing to look forward to.
    2b I feel that I won't ever get over my troubles.
    3 I feel that the future is hopeless and that things cannot improve.

C. (Sense of failure)
    0 I do not feel like a failure.
    1 I feel I have failed more than the average person.
    2a I feel I have accomplished very little that is worthwhile or that means anything.
    2b As I look back on my life all I can see is a lot of failures.
    3 I feel I am a complete failure as a person (parent, husband, wife).

D. (Dissatisfaction)
    0 I am not particularly dissatisfied.
    1a I feel bored most of the time.
    1b I don't enjoy things the way I used to.
    2 I don't get satisfaction out of anything anymore.
    3 I am dissatisfied with everything.

E. (Guilt)
    0 I don't feel particularly guilty.
    1 I feel bad or unworthy a good part of the time.
    2a I feel quite guilty.
    2b I feel bad or unworthy practically all the time now.
    3 I feel as though I am very bad or worthless.

F. (Expectation of punishment)
    0 I don't feel I am being punished.
    1 I have a feeling that something bad may happen to me.
    2 I feel I am being punished or will be punished.
    3a I feel I deserve to be punished.
    3b I want to be punished.

G. (Self-dislike)
    0 I don't feel disappointed in myself.
    1a I am disappointed in myself.
    1b I don't like myself.
    2 I am disgusted with myself.
    3 I hate myself.

H. (Self-accusations)
    0 I don't feel I am any worse than anybody else.
    1 I am critical of myself for my weaknesses or mistakes.
    2 I blame myself for my faults.
    3 I blame myself for everything bad that happens.

I. (Suicidal ideas)
    0 I don't have any thoughts of harming myself.
    1 I have thoughts of harming myself but I would not carry them out.
    2a I feel I would be better off dead.
    2b I feel my family would be better off if I were dead.
    3a I have definite plans about committing suicide.
    3b I would kill myself if I could.

J. (Crying)
    0 I don't cry any more than usual.
    1 I cry more now than I used to.
    2 I cry all the time now. I can't stop it.
    3 I used to be able to cry but now I can't cry at all even though I want to.

K. (Irritability)
    0 I am no more irritated now than I ever am.
    1 I get annoyed or irritated more easily than I used to.
    2 I feel irritated all the time.
    3 I don't get irritated at all at the things that used to irritate me.

L. (Social withdrawal)
    0 I have not lost interest in other people.
    1 I am less interested in other people now than I used to be.
    2 I have lost most of my interest in other people.
    3 I have lost all my interest in other people and don't care about them at all.

M. (Indecisiveness)
    0 I make decisions about as well as ever.
    1 I try to put off making decisions.
    2 I have great difficulty in making decisions.
    3 I can't make decisions at all anymore.

N. (Body image change)
    0 I don't feel I look any worse than I used to.
    1 I am worried that I am looking old or unattractive.
    2 I feel that there are permanent changes in my appearance and they make me look unattractive.
    3 I feel that I am ugly or repulsive-looking.

O. (Work retardation)
    0 I can work about as well as before.
    1a It takes extra effort to get started at doing.
    1b I don't work as well as I used to.
    2 I have to push myself very hard to do anything.
    3 I can't do any work at all.

P. (Insomnia)
    0 I can sleep as well as usual.
    1 I wake up more tired in the morning than I used to.
    2 I wake up 1–2 hours earlier than usual and find it hard to get back to sleep.
    3 I wake up early every day and can't get more than 5 hours sleep.

Q. (Fatigability)
    0 I don't get any more tired than usual.
    1 I get tired more easily than I used to.
    2 I get tired from doing anything.
    3 I get too tired to do anything.

R. (Anorexia)
    0 My appetite is no worse than usual.
    1 My appetite is not as good as it used to be.
    2 My appetite is much worse now.
    3 I have no appetite at all anymore.

S. (Weight loss)
    0 I haven't lost much weight, if any, lately.
    1 I have lost more than 5 pounds.
    2 I have lost more than 10 pounds.
    3 I have lost more than 15 pounds.

T. (Somatic preoccupation)
    0 I am no more concerned about my health than usual.
    1 I am concerned about aches and pains or upset stomach or constipation.
    2 I am so concerned with how I feel or what I feel that it's hard to think of much else.
    3 I am completely absorbed in what.I feel.

U. (Loss of libido)
    0 I have not noticed any recent change in my interest in sex.
    1 I am less interested in sex than I used to be.
    2 I am much less interested in sex now.
    3 I have lost interest in sex completely.

SCORING THE INVENTORY

Your score for each item is the *highest* number that you've circled for any of the statements within that group. That is, if you circled 1 for group "A. (Sadness)," your score for A would be 1 point. If you circled more than one statement in a group, your score for that item would be only the highest number you circled. For example, if for "B. (Pessimism)" you circled both statements 1 and 2b, your score for item B would be two points. To get your total score for the test, add up your points for each item. Thus your total score is made up of 21 individual item scores and can range from zero to 63 points. Write your score in the box below.

**TOTAL
SCORE**

INTERPRETING YOUR SCORE

Low Scorers (0–5)—If you scored in this range, you probably took this test for fun. Your answers indicate that you are showing almost no signs of feeling depressed. Hopefully, your score also means that you're feeling quite good about yourself and the world around you. If, however, things don't seem as right with your life as this low score suggests, depression may not be the best label for what you are experiencing. You may pick up on your problem area better by taking some of the tests in the other chapters of *The Mind Test*. Keep in mind also that this test asks for how you are feeling right this minute. If today just happens to be a great day, you may find it helpful to take this test again at another time.

Medium Scorers (6–14)—Scores in this range usually indicate a mild to moderate level of depression. You may feel "down" often enough to make life less enjoyable than it could be but not enough to have you generally feeling bad. This level of depression also suggests that there may be times when it's hard for you to find enough energy to make it through the day. This is a common problem for many of us, since almost everyone shows mild levels of depression at one time or another. That knowledge may not, however, make you feel any better. To help you understand your own level of depression, look over those items that produced your score with particular attention to any on which you scored 2 or 3. Think about how these symptoms relate to the way your life is going, and see if you can identify particular parts of your life that have you down. If you scored at the high end of this range, it's likely that there are important areas in your life causing you serious concern. Many of the professionally written self-help programs are designed to provide you with techniques for understanding and changing some of these problem areas. If you cannot identify the problems or if they seem overwhelming to you, you may gain the most benefit from professional help. It is likely that you are feeling bad enough to have to acknowledge your pain, but you probably also have enough energy to make treatment productive.

High Scorers (15 and above)—If you scored 15 or higher, you did not need this test to describe your current feelings as a possibly severe level of depression. You no doubt were well aware of how down you felt before you answered any of the questions. In fact, it's a positive sign that you were interested enough in self-understanding and had enough energy to take this test. If you scored fairly high, you probably see most things in your life as a waste of time or just too much trouble. And the future doesn't look very bright. Since you've taken this one important step toward understanding your problems, continue that self-help direction by getting in touch with your physician or a psychologist or other mental health professional; depression at this level does not often go away without help.

ABOUT THE INVENTORY

The Beck Depression Inventory is an example of how tests can be developed directly from a psychiatrist's or psychologist's clinical experiences. During the early 1950s psychiatrist Aaron T. Beck became interested in measuring depression. As part of a combination research and clinical treatment program, Dr. Beck worked with five soldiers who had become psychotically depressed after having accidentally killed a comrade. His evaluation of their concerns and emotional problems convinced him of the need for more accurate ways to assess depression than were available at that time.

As Dr. Beck continued his work with people being seen clinically for depression, he began developing specific test items to measure the kinds of feelings and behaviors that psychiatrists and psychologists observed during clinical interviews. You will notice as you look over the twenty-one items that each of them has a label that represents a symptom of depression. An important part of your own test score interpretation will be an examination of those symptoms for which you scored the highest. Dr. Beck's research has established how each symptom is related to overall levels of depression. Some—sadness, pessimism, and dissatisfaction, for example—have a high relationship to overall levels of depression. Others, such as irritability and weight loss, are meaningful but less related specifically to depression. Ones such as suicidal thoughts are correlated with depression levels but also extremely significant in their own right.

Desire for Novelty Scale

by Pamela H. Pearson

Below you will find a series of statements about feelings which may or may not be characteristic of you. If the statement accurately describes you, indicate this by circling "Like me." If the statement does not describe you accurately, circle "Unlike me." If you are uncertain how to answer an item, your first inclination is best. Take the test before reading further.

---

1. I wish something new and exciting would happen.   Like me   Unlike me

2. I feel that life is boring.   Like me   Unlike me

3. I wish I were doing something new and different.   Like me   Unlike me

4. I wish for some major change in my life.   Like me   Unlike me

5. I often feel that I am in a rut.   Like me   Unlike me

6. I experience life as just the same old thing from day to day.   Like me   Unlike me

7. I often wish life were more stimulating.   Like me   Unlike me

8. I often feel that everything is tiresome and dull.   Like me   Unlike me

9. I wish I could change places with someone who lived an exciting life.   Like me   Unlike me

10. I often wish life were different than it is.   Like me   Unlike me

Pearson, P. H. Relationships between global and specified measures of novelty seeking. *Journal of Consulting and Clinical Psychology*, 1970, *34*, Table 2, p. 201. Copyright 1970 by the American Psychological Association. Reprinted by permission.

SCORING THE SCALE

Your score is the number of times you circled "Like me" as your answer. Put that total score in the box at the bottom of the answer column.

INTERPRETING YOUR SCORE

Low Scorers (0–5)—Low scorers on this scale are describing themselves as generally content with the way things are in their lives at present. If you scored here, your low desire for novelty and change could be the result of self-examination which has led to a positive view of who you are and what you are doing. On the other hand, a low score could be a statement that life has been too hectic recently and that you would now like to move into calmer times. Give some thought to how these two interpretations fit with your own low desire for novelty.

High Scorers (6–10)—As a high scorer, you are expressing a wish for new experiences and stating that you are not satisfied with the status quo. Such a score could be a report of boredom or depression with a life that is not as meaningful or exciting as you would like. Perhaps you can handle this desire for novelty with simple life changes, such as taking a different route to work or eating out in a new restaurant. If your desire is intense, however, you will benefit from critical reflection about what you want in life. Rather than a new route to work, you may really want a new job. But such life changes, particularly as reactions to possible depressive feelings, bring stress and anxiety along with novelty, and need to be clearly analyzed in advance.

ABOUT THE SCALE

Many psychological tests come from the desire to take a global, ambiguous concept and attempt to specify what it is that makes up that concept. Such was the situation and ambition for psychologist Pamela Pearson. Dr. Pearson's work with the concepts of human novelty seeking and exploratory behavior achieved for her and colleague Dr. Donald Fiske a research grant from the National Science Foundation. One of the scales produced by Dr. Pearson is the Desire for Novelty Scale we have included here.

This scale measures a desire for new experiences that, for many people, is related to day-to-day levels of energy and enthusiasm for life. Psychologists are well aware of the relationship between low energy for new activities and feelings of depression. A major factor in depression is a sense of apathy, fatigue, and boredom with life. The writer-director-producer Paddy Chayefsky dramatized these feelings in his movie *Marty*, where two men hanging out on a Saturday night keep asking each other:

What do you want to do, Marty?
I don't know. What do you want to do, Angie?
I don't know, Marty. What do you want to do?

Self-Rating Depression Scale

by William K. Zung

Below are twenty statements about feelings each of us has at one time or another. Read each one and place a check in the box which best describes how you are feeling at this time.

	A little of the time	Some of the time	Good part of the time	Most of the time	
1. I feel downhearted and blue.					1.
2. Morning is when I feel best.					2.
3. I have crying spells or feel like it.					3.
4. I have trouble sleeping at night.					4.
5. I eat as much as I used to.					5.
6. I still enjoy sex.					6.
7. I notice that I am losing weight.					7.
8. I have trouble with constipation.					8.
9. My heart beats faster than usual.					9.
10. I get tired for no reason.					10.
11. My mind is as clear as it used to be.					11.
12. I find it easy to do the things I used to do.					12.
13. I am restless and can't keep still.					13.
14. I feel hopeful about the future.					14.
15. I am more irritable than usual.					15.
16. I find it easy to make decisions.					16.
17. I feel that I am useful and needed.					17.
18. My life is pretty full.					18.
19. I feel that others would be better off if I were dead.					19.
20. I still enjoy the things I used to do.					20.

ABOUT THE SCALE

Whether we describe it as feeling blue, or hopeless, or withdrawn, we have each experienced what psychologists label depression. In fact, depression has been called by psychologists the "common cold of psychopathology." Of all the emotional problems available to us, depression is one of the most common. We have all experienced the depression from the loss of a loved one, from separation from our friends, or from our failures. Such depression is normal and, being normal, it is usually transitory and specific to a certain situation. The important thing for us to know about our depressive feelings is the level and pervasiveness of those feelings. A scale which gives us that knowledge can be very beneficial.

A similar need led psychiatrist William Zung to develop his Self-Rating Depression Scale. During a research project measuring the relationship of depression and arousal during sleep, Dr. Zung found the available measures of depression inadequate. He wrote, "These inadequacies related to factors such as the length of a scale being too long and too time-consuming, especially for a patient who is already depressed and having psychomotor difficulties." His model for a scale required that it be easily completed by the person involved, and that it serve as an accurate measure of how the person was feeling at that particular time.

SCORING THE SCALE

Fold this page back along the dotted line and compare your answers to the key below. Circle the points corresponding to each of the boxes you have checked on the scale. Add up the total points and place that score in the box below.

TOTAL SCORE

	A little of the time	Some of the time	Good part of the time	Most of the time
1.	1	2	4	4
2.	4	3	2	1
3.	1	2	3	4
4.	1	2	3	4
5.	4	3	2	1
6.	4	3	2	1
7.	1	2	3	4
8.	1	2	3	4
9.	1	2	3	4
10.	1	2	3	4
11.	4	3	2	1
12.	4	3	2	1
13.	1	2	3	4
14.	4	3	2	1
15.	1	2	3	4
16.	4	3	2	1
17.	4	3	2	1
18.	4	3	2	1
19.	1	2	3	4
20.	4	3	2	1

FOLD BACK TO SCORE

INTERPRETING YOUR SCORE

Low Scorers (20–32)—If you scored in this range, you are scoring similar to Dr. Zung's original group of nondepressed people. You are reporting the opposite of those feelings expressed by people feeling depressed. For you, this means feelings of energy, hopefulness, and health. This isn't to say that you never feel depressed. As we said earlier, we all do at one time or another. But for now, the world looks bright to you, and that no doubt makes it easier for you to have fun.

Medium Scorers (33–50)—Medium scorers are reporting mild to moderate feelings of depression, probably encompassing several problem areas such as sleep, energy, and enjoyment of life. Your level of depression, depending on how high in this range you scored, is not one to be taken lightly. This is particularly true if you can't pinpoint any reasons for feeling as you do. But mild levels of depression sometimes respond well to concentrated self-help programs, such as those dealing with social skills training, relaxation, or techniques to increase pleasant activities. If your energy level is too low for such programs or if your depression has been going on for some time, seek professional help.

High Scorers (51–80)—People who score high on this scale are reporting a potentially severe level of depression. If you scored here, regard this as something that needs to be dealt with right away. There is little doubt that life for you now is not much fun. It may even mean that during the times you feel the most down, you've had fleeting thoughts of suicide. Such thoughts are common during severe depression, but they are a signal that says professional help is immediately required. Use the energy you've gotten together to take this test to arrange for at least a first meeting with a psychologist or other mental health professional.

Generalized Contentment Scale

by Walter W. Hudson

This questionnaire is designed to measure the degree of contentment that you feel about your life and surroundings. It is not a test, so there are no right or wrong answers. Answer each item as carefully and accurately as you can by placing a number beside each one as follows:

1 = Rarely or none of the time

2 = A little of the time

3 = Some of the time

4 = A good part of the time

5 = Most or all of the time

_____ 1. I feel powerless to do anything about my life.

_____ 2. I feel blue.

_____ 3. I am restless and can't keep still.

_____ 4. I have crying spells.

_____ 5. It is easy for me to relax.

_____ 6. I have a hard time getting started on things that I need to do.

_____ 7. I do not sleep well at night.

_____ 8. When things get tough, I feel there is always someone I can turn to.

_____ 9. I feel that the future looks bright for me.

_____ 10. I feel downhearted.

_____ 11. I feel that I am needed.

_____ 12. I feel that I am appreciated by others.

_____ 13. I enjoy being active and busy.

_____ 14. I feel that others would be better off without me.

_____ 15. I enjoy being with other people.

_____ 16. I feel it is easy for me to make decisions.

_____ 17. I feel downtrodden.

_____ 18. I am irritable.

_____ 19. I get upset easily.

_____ 20. I feel that I don't deserve to have a good time.

_____ 21. I have a full life.

_____ 22. I feel that people really care about me.

_____ 23. I have a great deal of fun.

_____ 24. I feel great in the morning.

_____ 25. I feel that my situation is hopeless.

SCORING KEY

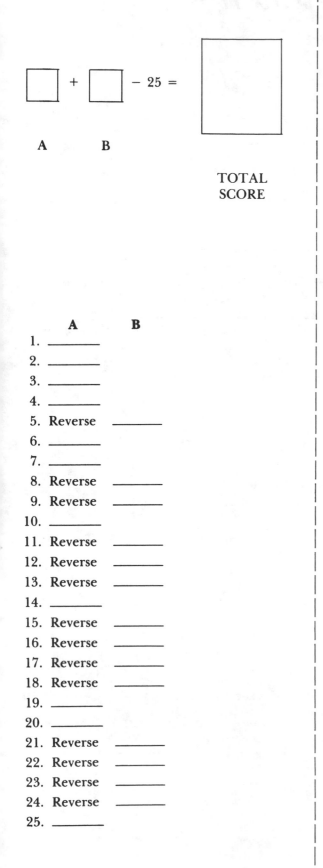

$$\boxed{} + \boxed{} - 25 = \boxed{\phantom{\text{TOTAL}}}$$

A   B

TOTAL SCORE

	A	B
1.	___	
2.	___	
3.	___	
4.	___	
5.	Reverse	___
6.	___	
7.	___	
8.	Reverse	___
9.	Reverse	___
10.	___	
11.	Reverse	___
12.	Reverse	___
13.	Reverse	___
14.	___	
15.	Reverse	___
16.	Reverse	___
17.	Reverse	___
18.	Reverse	___
19.	___	
20.	___	
21.	Reverse	___
22.	Reverse	___
23.	Reverse	___
24.	Reverse	___
25.	___	

FOLD BACK TO SCORE

SCORING THE SCALE

To score this scale fold this page back along the dotted line and compare your answers with those on the Scoring Key.

First, transfer your answers into the spaces in Column A for items 1, 2, 3, 4, etc. Next, in Column B, reverse the numerical value of your answer for items 5, 8, 9, 11, etc. For example:

In Column B an answer of

    1 earns 5 points

    2 earns 4 points

    3 earns 3 points

    4 earns 2 points

    5 earns 1 point

To find your final score, add together the total points in Column A and the total points in Column B. From this sum subtract 25 points. The result is your final score.

INTERPRETING YOUR SCORE

Below Average Scores (0–29)—People who score in this range are reporting moderate to very high contentment with life as they see it at present. For you this suggests that even if there are some rough spots on a day-to-day basis they aren't enough to depress your positive view of life. It's likely that you have the energy needed to smooth out any problems that you come across. If you scored in the upper part of this range and find some of the earlier discussion about depression applicable to you, give some serious examination to depression as a problem for you at this time. If it is high enough to worry you (regardless of your score), do something about it, such as have a talk with a friend, enter a self-change program, or get professional help. If you scored very low on the scale, then the sky's the limit for you; life looks, and probably is, great.

Above Average Scores (30–100)—The score of 30 is used as the start of the high range because of Dr. Hudson's research which showed scores of 30 and above to be highly related to complaints of depression. If you scored here, it is very likely that you are aware of your depressive feelings and behaviors. Since depression can be a relatively short-lived and situation-specific problem, however, scores in the lower part of this range may stem from acute life concerns. As your score increases, your report of unhappiness, apathy, and self-doubt also increases. Regardless of what may be causing your depression, higher scores indicate the need for professional contact. Such help can mean less intense negative feelings and an overall shorter period of depression. Your physician or mental health professional is a good place to start.

ABOUT THE SCALE

This chapter contains several ways of measuring the unpleasant emotional experiences categorized as depression. Each technique looks at slightly different aspects of depression, from the desire for new experiences to physical ailments and self-doubt. In his review of available measures of depression in 1974, Dr. Walter Hudson pointed out that most instruments measured primarily symptomatic or behavioral manifestations of depression, leaving out the more personal, cognitive thoughts of the individual. He saw the need for a scale directed toward the client's thoughts and feelings about how his life is going—in essence, his degree of contentment with life. Dr. Hudson wrote, "it seems apparent that another device designed to measure and quantify depressive affect would be a welcome addition to clinical treatment and research."

His work led to the development of the Generalized Contentment Scale, twenty-five items designed "to measure the feelings of the respondent about a number of behaviors, attitudes, events, affect states, and cognitions that are associated with depression." It was important that the scale be brief enough so as not to appear overwhelming to someone taking it. Since clinicians know that low levels of energy and enthusiasm are part of depression, a long test would require too much effort from the very person who needed to take it. Thus his scale is brief (usually completed in three to five minutes), contains minimal instructions, and has straightforward questions. It appears to meet Dr. Hudson's goals for a new device designed to measure certain aspects of depression.

CHAPTER SEVEN

Vocation

A psychologist recently described his client, Mary Ellen, who worked for six years as a legal secretary: After noting how hard she worked and how uninterested she had become, the psychologist gave her a vocational interest test. The test results, along with Mary Ellen's reflections during the test-interpretation counseling session, led her to take the L.S.A.T.—Law School Aptitude Test. To her astonishment, she made a very rare, near-perfect score. Despite mediocre grades as an undergraduate, she was admitted into law school and is now a practicing attorney. In Mary Ellen's case, a vocational interest test combined with her ability to do well on a law aptitude test made a major difference in her life.

One does not have to be dissatisfied with one's job or profession to effectively use a battery of vocational tests. The young man or woman fresh out of college can use vocational testing to eliminate bad choices, indicate new options, or encourage previous interests. Conversely, it is not unusual for an individual to decide to make a midlife career change—often, just for the sake of change. Through testing a lawyer might find she is happier working as a carpenter or architect; a nurse may discover he has a high aptitude for numbers and switch to accounting. The first rule in finding a suitable vocation is to know how your own abilities and interests match the requirements of the work.

Different tasks require different abilities. One phenomenon which demonstrated the importance of vocational aptitudes was the computer revolution. In the nineteen-sixties, when computer programmers, operators, and analysts were needed by the tens of thousands, the "computer bums" made their appearance. It turned out that a few people who weren't particularly distinguished in other fields—many of them, in fact, were regarded as failures or misfits—demonstrated remarkable abilities as programmers. The nature of computer programming requires the kind of mind that is analytical and logical, capable of breaking up complex tasks into small steps, then assembling those steps into a coherent whole. This is the kind of very specific aptitude and interest pattern that can be detected by written tests.

Vocational tests can be equally useful in finding an avocation. You may be relatively satisfied with your employment but feel that you need something more in your life. If your vocational tests reveal an interest in working with your hands, a hobby such as carpentry or playing the piano can enhance that empty space in your life. If you demonstrate an aptitude for colors, shapes, and design, painting could be a fulfilling avocation. The major goal of vocational testing is to uncover which areas of work match your interests and which of your abilities are your strongest. This can be revealing and helpful information no matter what your job status may be.

Interest Check List

by the United States Department of Labor

Beginning below are 115 activities listed in 23 groups. Read each activity and place a check next to those that you would like as jobs or hobbies. Check an activity even if you are interested in only one part of it. If you have not done an activity but think that you would like to, given the opportunity, check that one also. If you are not interested in the activities in any one group, leave a blank. Work quickly by not spending too much time thinking about any one kind of work.

A

_____ Sketching and painting portraits, landscapes, still life or figures on canvas

_____ Creating, designing and painting posters, signboards, showcards, charts, diagrams, labels, and illustrations for advertising copy, books, and magazines

_____ Modeling or carving various objects from wood, clay, plaster, or stone

_____ Sketching rooms and planning the arrangement of furniture, wall decorations, and color schemes

_____ Creating and drawing to scale patterns for new types and styles of clothes

B

_____ Playing a musical instrument

_____ Singing various types of songs

_____ Creating and composing musical compositions or arranging a melody for orchestral use

_____ Conducting an orchestra

_____ Studying musical theory and techniques, melody, and harmony

C

_____ Writing magazine articles, plays, short stories, poems or books

_____ Translating from one language to another

_____ Reporting news for a newspaper or magazine

_____ Writing or editing news items for a newspaper, periodical, or book

_____ Doing literary research for historical publications

D

_____ Acting in a play or dramatic production

_____ Announcing radio programs

_____ Dancing for the entertainment of others

_____ Making a living by playing football, baseball, hockey, or other sports

_____ Entertaining others by juggling, sleight-of-hand, pantomime, or magic

E

_____ Developing advertising campaigns

_____ Applying the principles of accounting, statistical analysis, contracts, credit, marketing conditions, and applied psychology to the problems of business

_____ Drawing up legal documents such as contracts, partnerships, deeds, and wills

_____ Conducting lawsuits

_____ Working up sales methods

F

_____ Figuring out arithmetic problems using multiplication, division, squares, and square roots

_____ Copying long lists of numbers and checking to be sure they are copied right

_____ Finding mistakes in answers to arithmetic problems

_____ Doing addition and subtraction

_____ Working with fractions and decimals

Reprinted in the public domain.

G

_____ Keeping business records, such as sales slips, receipts, bills, attendance records, and amount of goods purchased or work done.

_____ Typing letters and reports

_____ Taking dictation in shorthand or on a stenotype machine

_____ Receiving, checking, counting, grading, examining, and storing supplies

_____ Sorting, indexing, and assembling papers and other written records

H

_____ Being a salesclerk, selling or taking tickets, handling money, or making change

_____ Answering the telephone

_____ Giving people information such as street directions or location of merchandise in stores

_____ Preparing lists of prospects and contacting them in order to make sales

_____ Attempting to interest prospective buyers by showing sample articles or displaying a catalog

I

_____ Teaching school

_____ Talking to individuals or families and assisting them in solving their personal or financial problems

_____ Interviewing and advising individuals concerning their schooling, jobs, and social problems

_____ Studying social and economic conditions in order to help individuals or groups solve problems of general welfare

_____ Enforcing laws involving fire and crime prevention, traffic, sanitation, or immigration

J

_____ Planning a balanced diet (planning a menu or a meal)

_____ Mixing foods to obtain new flavor

_____ Going to some trouble to make foods look attractive

_____ Learning the right way to season foods

_____ Selecting meats and vegetables in a grocery store for freshness and quality

K

_____ Playing games with children

_____ Telling stories to children

_____ Looking after children to see that they are kept neat and clean

_____ Taking care of children when they are sick

_____ Helping children dress or undress

L

_____ Giving first aid treatment

_____ Setting tables and serving food or drinks

_____ Acting as a hostess or headwaiter in a dining room

_____ Caring for people's hair and fixing their nails

_____ Waiting on other people and caring for their clothes

M

_____ Studying the soils, weather, climate, and so on in which plants and animals live and grow best

_____ Plowing, planting, cultivating, or harvesting crops

_____ Trying out various methods of growing plants to find the best way

_____ Breeding, raising, and caring for livestock such as cattle, sheep, hogs, and chickens

N

_____ Catching fish with nets, hooks, harpoons, spears, or guns

_____ Cleaning fish

_____ Steering ships and plotting a course with the aid of a compass or sextant

_____ Standing watch on a ship to look out for rocks, lighthouses, buoys, or other ships

_____ Observing activity of fish to determine their habits and food requirements

O

_____ Using a trap to catch animals

_____ Acting as a guide for hunting parties

_____ Chopping or sawing down trees and trimming branches from trees using an ax or saw

_____ Moving or piling up stacks of logs and loading and fastening logs with chains

_____ Caring for forests by looking out for fires or tree diseases

P

_____ Designing machinery and mechanical or electrical equipment

_____ Developing and executing plans for the construction of buildings or bridges

_____ Using drafting tools to prepare detailed plans and drawings for buildings or machines

_____ Doing research in a chemical, physical, or biological laboratory

_____ Drawing maps

Q

_____ Taking apart mechanical things such as bicycles, automobile engines, pumps, typewriters, or guns and putting them back together again

_____ Examining mechanical equipment for wear or damaged parts to see what needs to be done

_____ Following complicated directions and diagrams to put parts of machines together

_____ Tuning up motors to see that they are running right

_____ Greasing and oiling machines

R

_____ Repairing electric stoves, refrigerators, vacuum cleaners, fans, and motors

_____ Studying the theory of electricity, including direct and alternating current, volts, amperes, ohms, etc.

_____ Wiring, splicing, soldering, and insulating electrical connections

_____ Building and testing radio sets

_____ Changing fuses, repairing electric irons, wiring lamps, fixing light plugs and short circuits

S

_____ Working on scaffolds and climbing around on buildings while assembling large pieces with a hammer, rivets, or welding equipment

_____ Painting, plastering, puttying, or paperhanging

_____ Working with hand tools such as saws, plumb lines, rulers, and squares

_____ Bending, threading, and fitting pipes, fixing drains and faucets

_____ Doing carpentry, plumbing, floor-laying, or roofing

T

_____ Assembling or repairing instruments such as watches, locks, cameras, fountain pens, or field glasses

_____ Examining, inspecting, and separating objects according to quality, size, color, or weight

_____ Cutting and shaping glass or stone for jewelry and similar small articles

_____ Cutting, shaping, and rolling dough for breads and pastries

_____ Cutting, sewing, or repairing clothing, shoes, or other articles from cloth, leather, or fur

U

_____ Running lathes, drill presses, and other machine shop equipment

_____ Making calculations to determine angles, curves, or shapes of small metal or wooden parts

_____ Pushing levers and buttons or turning handwheels to start, stop, slow down or speed up machines

_____ Operating heavy equipment to move dirt or rocks

_____ Making parts and tools from metal

V

_____ Doing freehand lettering or copying sketches on wood, metal, canvas, or film

_____ Making photographic copies of drawings, records, or pictures for books or newspapers

_____ Setting type by hand or machine for printing, or working with sizes, styles, and spacing of type or proofreading

_____ Using soft crayon to copy maps, charts, posters, and drawings

_____ Cutting designs or letters into metal, stone, or glass, using hand tools or engraving wheels

W

_____ Observing formulas, timing, temperature, and pressure directions

_____ Handling or pouring hot metals, or plating metals

_____ Operating furnaces, boilers, ovens, and other equipment

_____ Grinding, mixing, or separating chemicals

_____ Measuring, mixing, or cooking foods for canning

ABOUT THE CHECK LIST

The Interest Check List was developed by the Occupational Analysis and Industrial Services Division of the U.S. Department of Labor. The check list's primary purpose is to serve as an interviewing aid when a counselor feels that further information on a counselee's interests is desired. As stated in the test manual, "It will be useful with persons who have no definite stated work interest or with those whose knowledge of the wide variety of tasks and activities which exist in the various occupational fields is limited."

The items and job categories used in the Interest Check List were taken from the *Dictionary of Occupational Titles*. This book groups thousands of jobs found in business and industry into a relatively small number of fields of work on the basis of interrelationships among jobs. These relationships may be in the materials or equipment used, the nature of the work performed, the amount and type of knowledge required, or other factors. The *Dictionary of Occupational Titles* is easily found in the reference section of your local library and can be useful in giving you added information about jobs which seem interesting.

SCORING THE CHECK LIST

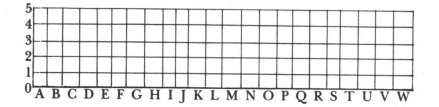

First, count the number of checks in each group of activities. Then darken the bar graph above, beginning at the bottom, up to the appropriate level in that letter group. If there are no checks in any one group, leave the bar blank. See the example below.

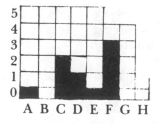

INTERPRETING YOUR SCORES

A   Artistic
B   Musical
C   Literary
D   Entertainment
E   Clerical and Sales: Technical Work
F   Clerical and Sales: Computing Work
G   Recording and General Clerical Work
H   Public Contact Work
I   Service Work: Public Service
J   Service Work: Cooking
K   Child Care
L   Personal Service
M   Farming
N   Marine
O   Forestry
P   Engineering: Technical Work
Q   Mechanical Work
R   Electrical Work
S   Structural Crafts
T   Bench Crafts
U   Machinery and Machine Operating
V   Graphic Art Work
W   Processing

High Categories. List the letters of your four *highest* groups below. Next to each letter write the job category associated with that letter from the above list.

___   _____
___   _____
___   _____
___   _____

By having these as your four highest categories, you are stating that, relative to all of the job characteristics listed, these are the most appealing to you. Look at the labels of these four categories and at the activities that make up those groups. Pay particular attention to any similarities among the types of activities involved. These labels describe certain jobs and job characteristics taken from vocational research.

Checking the activities as you have done ranks these as important to you in your own vocational choice. If you have more than four groups high in number of checks, you are reporting a diversified interest pattern which probably allows you to choose from many jobs that will provide high satisfaction. Your highest level of job satisfaction will come from a position that allows you to be involved in as many of the checked activities as possible.

Low Categories. List the letters of your four *lowest* groups below. Next to each letter write the job category listed with that letter above.

___   _____
___   _____
___   _____
___   _____

By ranking these as your lowest categories, you are reporting little interest in having these activities involved in your job or hobbies. You would likely be unhappy if you were to have a job that stressed these activities. If, however, your job were also to emphasize areas in which you scored high, your satisfaction would depend on the intensity of your likes and dislikes for these activities. If you find yourself having a job that does involve low ranked activities, involving yourself in hobbies that stress high-ranked ones may increase your overall satisfaction with work.

Telic Dominance Scale

by Stephen Murgatroyd, Cyril Rushton,
Michale Apter, and Colette Ray

ANSWER COLUMN
A or B

On the next page are 42 pairs of activities. Select the alternative within each pair that you would prefer, or that most nearly applies to the way you see yourself. Mark your choice by placing an (a) or (b) in the answer column.

1. _____
2. _____
3. _____
4. _____
5. _____
6. _____
7. _____
8. _____
9. _____
10. _____
11. _____
12. _____
13. _____
14. _____
15. _____
16. _____
17. _____
18. _____
19. _____
20. _____
21. _____
22. _____
23. _____
24. _____
25. _____
26. _____
27. _____
28. _____
29. _____
30. _____
31. _____
32. _____
33. _____
34. _____
35. _____
36. _____
37. _____
38. _____
39. _____
40. _____
41. _____
42. _____

1. a. Compile a short dictionary for financial reward
   b. Write a short story for fun
2. a. Going to evening class to improve your qualifications
   b. Going to evening class for fun
3. a. Improving a sporting skill by playing a game
   b. Improving it through systematic practice
4. a. Work that earns promotion
   b. Work that you enjoy doing
5. a. Planning your leisure
   b. Doing things on the spur of the moment
6. a. Going to formal evening meetings
   b. Watching television for entertainment
7. a. Investing money in a long-term insurance/pension scheme
   b. Buying an expensive car
8. a. Spending $200 having an enjoyable weekend
   b. Spending $200 repaying a loan
9. a. Fixing long-term life ambitions
   b. Living life as it comes
10. a. Always trying to finish your work before you enjoy yourself
    b. Frequently going out for enjoyment before all your work is finished
11. a. Not needing to explain your behavior
    b. Having purposes for your behavior
12. a. Playing a game
    b. Organizing a game
13. a. Planning ahead
    b. Taking each day as it comes
14. a. Planning a holiday
    b. Being on holiday
15. a. Leisure activities which are just exciting
    b. Leisure activities which have a purpose
16. a. Spending one's life in many different places
    b. Spending most of one's life in one place
17. a. Having your tasks set for you
    b. Choosing your own activities
18. a. Staying in one job
    b. Having many changes of job
19. a. Seldom doing things "for kicks"
    b. Often doing things "for kicks"
20. a. Taking holidays in many different places
    b. Taking holidays always in the same place

21. a. Frequently trying strange foods
    b. Always eating familiar foods
22. a. Recounting an incident accurately
    b. Exaggerating for effect
23. a. Having continuity in the place where you live
    b. Having frequent moves of house
24. a. Taking risks
    b. Going through life safely
25. a. Winning a game easily
    b. Playing a game with scores very close
26. a. Steady routine in life
    b. Continual unexpectedness or surprise
27. a. Working in the garden
    b. Picking wild fruit
28. a. Traveling a great deal in one's job
    b. Working in one office or workshop
29. a. Going to a party
    b. Going to a meeting
30. a. Leisure activities
    b. Work activities
31. a. Going away on holiday for two weeks
    b. Given two weeks of free time finishing a needed improvement at home
32. a. Taking life seriously
    b. Treating life light-heartedly
33. a. Going to an art gallery to enjoy the exhibits
    b. To learn about the exhibits
34. a. Watching a game
    b. Refereeing a game
35. a. Eating special things because you enjoy them
    b. Eating special things because they are good for your health
36. a. Climbing a mountain to try to save someone
    b. Climbing a mountain for pleasure
37. a. Happy to waste time
    b. Always having to be busy
38. a. Watching a crucial match between two ordinary teams
    b. Watching an exhibition game with star performers
39. a. Glancing at pictures in a book
    b. Reading a biography
40. a. Reading for information
    b. Reading for fun
41. a. Arguing for fun
    b. Arguing with others seriously to change their opinions
42. a. Winning a game
    b. Playing a game for fun

SCORING KEY

1. a _____
2. a _____
3. b _____
4. a _____
5. a _____
6. a _____
7. a _____
8. b _____
9. a _____
10. a _____
11. b _____
12. b _____
13. a _____
14. a _____
15. b _____
16. b _____
17. a _____
18. a _____
19. a _____
20. b _____
21. b _____
22. a _____
23. a _____
24. b _____
25. a _____
26. a _____
27. a _____
28. b _____
29. b _____
30. b _____
31. b _____
32. a _____
33. b _____
34. b _____
35. b _____
36. a _____
37. b _____
38. a _____
39. b _____
40. a _____
41. b _____
42. a _____

TOTAL 1–14

☐

PLANNING ORIENTATION

TOTAL 15–28

☐

AROUSAL AVOIDANCE

TOTAL 29–42

☐

SERIOUS-MINDEDNESS

FOLD BACK TO SCORE

SCORING THE SCALE

To find your score, fold the Scoring Key back along the dotted line and compare your answers to those on the key. Give yourself one point for each match.

The test is actually divided into three subsets, so to compute your final scores, add the total for questions 1 through 14 and note it in the appropriate box. Repeat this process for questions 15 through 28, and questions 29 through 42.

INTERPRETING YOUR SCORE

The three personality characteristics of serious-mindedness, planning orientation, and arousal avoidance can be important considerations in job satisfaction. The issue is not just whether you are high or low on one or all of these traits; it is, rather, how your level of each of these relates to the degree that that characteristic is required for your present or potential job. To best interpret your scores, first read the description of each of the subscales. Think about how that trait is involved in your job. Then look at your own score for each of the characteristics and relate your level of each to your job's requirements. It is important to note, as the scale's authors have, that research with the Telic Dominance Scale has shown that these questions do not measure neuroticism. Interpret your scores, therefore, not as good or bad, but rather in terms of how your characteristics match those needed in your vocational situation.

Planning Orientation. These questions measure how much an individual plans ahead and organizes in pursuit of goals rather than taking things as they come. High scorers are oriented toward the future and gain pleasure from the planning for goals as well as from anticipated achievement. Low scorers, on the other hand, are "here-and-now" oriented, wanting pleasure from immediate behavior rather than from things sometime in the future. Very high scorers may be regarded as too future-oriented by friends and work colleagues, perhaps to the point of being seen as rigid and nonspontaneous. Jobs that involve long-range program development or that hold out the possibility of future success (even at the sacrifice of present rewards) fit with high levels of planning orientation.

Arousal Avoidance. This scale measures the degree to which an individual avoids situations that generate stimulation or high arousal. If you scored high on this subscale, you probably seek out situations that have low arousal levels, such as jobs that require little travel, have a fixed schedule, and have a clear set of responsibilities. High scorers are generally more comfortable being able to predict their daily routines than having a life full of surprises. Low scorers are inclined toward change and adapt easily to new situations.

Serious-mindedness. This subscale measures the degree to which you are oriented toward goals which you see as important to yourself or those close to you. High scorers tend to be business- or work-oriented rather than into activities just for fun. They also avoid spending energy for goals which are seen as arbitrary or inessential. Jobs that primarily involve intellectual tasks fit well with high levels of this trait.

ABOUT THE SCALE

How our jobs' demands match our personality characteristics has much to do with our job satisfaction and our job success. If you have a job, for example, that requires extreme attention to detail, but your personality is that of a happy-go-lucky person, sooner or later the difference will lead to unhappiness with your work. Such unhappiness affects both your job satisfaction and your overall view of life. In fact, vocational counseling emphasizes the need for understanding the job's personality as well as the employee's if the two are to produce a mutually satisfying match.

Though not specifically designed for use in vocational counseling, the Telic Dominance Scale measures three personality areas which are important in job-related activities and satisfaction. This scale was designed by its authors to measure aspects of telic dominance or "a state of mind in which the individual sees himself as pursuing some essential goal (telic), versus a focus on immediate sensations, on the here and now (pantelic)." In essense, the telic state focuses on the future while the pantelic orientation is on the present. Thus someone who, given the choice, would rather do something just for fun than do it because it was necessary would have a pantelic orientation. The scale authors selected three areas to measure using the telic-pantelic conceptualization. These characteristics are serious-mindedness, planning orientation, and arousal avoidance, and are discussed in the interpretation section for this scale. Each of these can be an important personality trait in vocational choice and job satisfaction.

Job Satisfaction Index

by BPC Publishing Ltd.

The questions below deal with your characteristics, attitudes, and feelings as they relate to your present job. Read each one carefully and decide which of the choices best describes you. Mark your answers in the answer column provided on the facing page.

1. Do you watch the clock when you are working?
   a. Constantly
   b. At slack times
   c. Never

2. When Monday morning comes, do you
   a. Feel ready to go back to work?
   b. Think longingly of being able to lie in the hospital with a broken leg?
   c. Feel reluctant to start with, but fit into the work routine quite happily after an hour or so?

3. How do you feel at the end of a working day?
   a. Dead tired and fit for nothing
   b. Glad that you can start living
   c. Sometimes tired, but usually pretty satisfied

4. Do you worry about your work?
   a. Occasionally
   b. Never
   c. Often

5. Would you say that your job
   a. Underuses your ability?
   b. Overstrains your abilities?
   c. Makes you do things you never thought you could do before?

6. Which statement is true for you?
   a. I am rarely bored with my work.
   b. I am usually interested in my work, but there are patches of boredom.
   c. I am bored most of the time I am working.

7. How much of your worktime is spent making personal telephone calls, or with other matters not connected with the job?
   a. Very little
   b. Some, especially at crisis times in my personal life
   c. Quite a lot

8. Do you daydream about having a different job?
   a. Very little
   b. Not a different job, but a better position in the same kind of job
   c. Yes

9. Would you say that you feel
   a. Pretty capable most of the time?
   b. Sometimes capable?
   c. Panicky and incapable most of the time?

10. Do you find that
    a. You like and respect your colleagues?
    b. You dislike your colleagues?
    c. You are indifferent to your colleagues?

11. Which statement is most true for you?
    a. I do not want to learn more about my work.
    b. I quite enjoyed learning my work when I first started.
    c. I like to go on learning as much as possible about my work.

12. Mark the qualities you think are your best points.
    a. Sympathy
    b. Clear-thinking
    c. Calmness
    d. Good memory
    e. Concentration
    f. Physical stamina
    g. Inventiveness
    h. Expertise
    i. Charm
    j. Humor

13. Now mark the above qualities that are demanded by your job.

14. Which statement do you most agree with?
    a. A job is only a way to make enough money to keep yourself alive.
    b. A job is mainly a way of making money, but should be satisfying if possible.
    c. A job is a whole way of life.

15. Do you work overtime?
    a. Only when it is paid
    b. Never
    c. Often, even without pay

16. Have you been absent from work (other than for normal vacations or illness) in the last year?
    a. Not at all
    b. For a few days only
    c. Often, even without pay

17. Would you rate yourself as
    a. Very ambitious?
    b. Unambitious?
    c. Mildly ambitious?

18. Do you think that your colleagues
    a. Like you, enjoy your company, and get on well with you in general?
    b. Dislike you?

c. Do not dislike you, but are not particularly friendly?

19. Do you talk about work
    a. Only with your colleagues?
    b. With friends and family?
    c. Not if you can avoid it?

20. Do you suffer from minor unexplained illnesses and vague pains?
    a. Seldom
    b. Not too often
    c. Frequently

21. How did you choose your present job?
    a. Your parents or teachers decided for you
    b. It was all you could find
    c. It seemed the right thing for you

22. In a conflict between job and home, like an illness of a member of the family, which would win?
    a. The family every time
    b. The job every time
    c. The family in a real emergency, but otherwise probably the job

23. Would you be happy to do the same job if it paid one third less?
    a. Yes
    b. You would like to, but could not afford to
    c. No

24. If you were made redundant, which of these would you miss most?
    a. The money
    b. The work itself
    c. The company of your colleagues

25. Would you take a day off to have fun?
    a. Yes
    b. No
    c. Possibly, if there was nothing too urgent for you to do at work

26. Do you feel unappreciated at work?
    a. Occasionally
    b. Often
    c. Rarely

27. What do you most dislike about your job?
    a. That your time is not your own
    b. The boredom
    c. That you cannot always do things the way you want to

28. Do you keep your personal life separate from work? (Check with your partner on this one.)
    a. Pretty strictly
    b. Most of the time, but there is some overlap
    c. Not at all

29. Would you advise a child of yours to take up the same kind of work as you do?
    a. Yes, if he had the ability and temperament
    b. No, you would warn him off
    c. You would not press it, but you would not discourage him either

30. If you won or suddenly inherited a large sum of money, would you
    a. Stop work for the rest of your life?
    b. Take up some kind of work that you have always wanted to do?
    c. Decide to continue, in some way, the same work you do now?

ANSWER COLUMN

1. a. _____ b. _____ c. _____
2. a. _____ b. _____ c. _____
3. a. _____ b. _____ c. _____
4. a. _____ b. _____ c. _____
5. a. _____ b. _____ c. _____
6. a. _____ b. _____ c. _____
7. a. _____ b. _____ c. _____
8. a. _____ b. _____ c. _____
9. a. _____ b. _____ c. _____
10. a. _____ b. _____ c. _____
11. a. _____ b. _____ c. _____
12. a. _____ b. _____ c. _____
    d. _____ e. _____ f. _____
    g. _____ h. _____ i. _____
    j. _____
13. a. _____ b. _____ c. _____
    d. _____ e. _____ f. _____
    g. _____ h. _____ i. _____
    j. _____
14. a. _____ b. _____ c. _____
15. a. _____ b. _____ c. _____
16. a. _____ b. _____ c. _____
17. a. _____ b. _____ c. _____
18. a. _____ b. _____ c. _____
19. a. _____ b. _____ c. _____
20. a. _____ b. _____ c. _____
21. a. _____ b. _____ c. _____
22. a. _____ b. _____ c. _____
23. a. _____ b. _____ c. _____
24. a. _____ b. _____ c. _____
25. a. _____ b. _____ c. _____
26. a. _____ b. _____ c. _____
27. a. _____ b. _____ c. _____
28. a. _____ b. _____ c. _____
29. a. _____ b. _____ c. _____
30. a. _____ b. _____ c. _____

SCORING THE INDEX

To find your score, fold this page forward on the dotted line and compare your answers to the Scoring Key. Give yourself the points listed for the choice you selected. Add those points together to get your total score and put that score in the box provided.

TOTAL SCORE

FOLD FORWARD TO SCORE

SCORING KEY

1.	a. 1	b. 3	c. 5
2.	a. 5	b. 1	c. 3
3.	a. 3	b. 1	c. 5
4.	a. 5	b. 3	c. 1
5.	a. 1	b. 3	c. 5
6.	a. 5	b. 3	c. 1
7.	a. 5	b. 3	c. 1
8.	a. 5	b. 3	c. 1
9.	a. 5	b. 3	c. 1
10.	a. 5	b. 3	c. 1
11.	a. 1	b. 3	c. 5

12 and 13. Score 5 each time you mark matching qualities

14.	a. 1	b. 3	c. 5
15.	a. 3	b. 1	c. 5
16.	a. 5	b. 3	c. 1
17.	a. 5	b. 1	c. 3
18.	a. 5	b. 1	c. 3
19.	a. 3	b. 5	c. 1
20.	a. 5	b. 3	c. 1
21.	a. 3	b. 1	c. 5
22.	a. 1	b. 5	c. 3
23.	a. 5	b. 3	c. 1
24.	a. 1	b. 5	c. 3
25.	a. 1	b. 5	c. 3
26.	a. 3	b. 1	c. 5
27.	a. 3	b. 1	c. 5
28.	a. 1	b. 3	c. 5
29.	a. 5	b. 1	c. 3
30.	a. 1	b. 3	c. 5

INTERPRETING YOUR SCORE

Low Scorers (28–80)—Your score here indicates that you are not generally satisfied with your present job. It does not, unfortunately, tell you what it is about your job that causes your unhappiness. Continued self-examination is needed to produce that information. Consider, however, that you may be in the wrong job for your interests or abilities. If that seems true for you, detailed vocational testing through a vocational counselor can provide you with a choice of jobs better suited to you as a person. Perhaps there are less major changes that you could make at work to increase your satisfaction. A talk with your boss or supervisor may enable you to shift your responsibilities to those more in keeping with your interests, or a change in location or colleagues may make a difference. Think carefully through any possible changes; the changes themselves can bring added stress if they are not what is really best for you.

Average Scorers (81–150)—Scores here represent the normal, solid level of satisfaction that most people have for their jobs. There is no doubt that there are things about your work that you would like to change, such as higher pay, better use of your skills, and less work-related stress. But, in general, you seem to have found a vocational area that is interesting to you, with colleagues who are an important part of your job satisfaction. You have most likely been able to strike a balance between your job and your personal life so that you can enjoy both.

High Scorers (151 and Above)—Your score in this range states that your work is very important to you and that you find it highly satisfying. You no doubt enjoy going to work so much that Monday may be the happiest day of the week for you. People who score very high in job satisfaction are committed to their jobs to the point of gaining much of their personal identity from their careers. Though this, in and of itself, is not a problem, such high commitment may mean that you base too much of your happiness on your job, perhaps to the exclusion of other areas of life that you would enjoy. An additional caution is that very high commitment may make you susceptible to problems resulting from work changes over which you have no control. You may find it useful to evaluate your job commitment and think about non-work activities that you would enjoy.

ABOUT THE INDEX

Workers today no longer care about their jobs the way they used to. Recent research points out that this is particularly true for younger workers, the very ones with the most flexibility in job choice. Many years ago job satisfaction and flexibility were more fantasy than real concerns. People went into jobs depending on where they lived and who their parents were. Today, however, greater educational and vocational opportunities allow us to be concerned with how much we like the jobs we have.

Psychologists involved in business and industry research have stressed the importance of job satisfaction in areas ranging from company productivity to the emotional health of the individual employee. Companies have found that programs evaluating and dealing with worker dissatisfaction lead to higher production, a decrease in job-related accidents, and fewer sick days. Individuals have found that when they gain a better understanding of their own feelings about their jobs, they are able to understand other day-to-day problems which may relate to job dissatisfaction. As part of their development of a series of behavioral science books, BPC Publishing Ltd. developed the Job Satisfaction Index which we have included here. Its primary purpose is that of providing you with an overview of your feelings toward your present job. There are many factors in addition to satisfaction that must be examined in choosing a career, such as aptitudes, goals, and opportunities. Job satisfaction, however, is a good place to start a self-examination of how you relate to your job.

The Quick Job-Hunting Map: The Party

by Richard N. Bolles

Below is an aerial view (from the floor above) of a room in which a party is taking place. At this party, people with the same or similar interests have (for some reason) all gathered in the same corners of the room. After looking over the room below, read the three questions at the bottom of the page and place your answers in the appropriate boxes.

AERIAL VIEW OF ROOM

R — People who have athletic or mechanical ability, prefer to work with objects, machines, tools, plants, or animals, or to be outdoors

I — People who like to observe, learn, investigate, analyze, evaluate, or solve problems

C — People who like to work with data, have clerical or numerical ability, carry things out in detail or follow through on others' instructions

A — People who have artistic, innovating, or intuitional abilities, and like to work in unstructured situations using their imaginations or creativity

E — People who like to work with people—influencing, persuading, performing, leading, or managing for organizational goals or for economic gain

S — People who like to work with people—to inform, enlighten, help, train, develop or cure them, or are skilled with words

1. Which corner of the room would you instinctively be drawn to as the group of people you would most *enjoy* being with for the longest time? (Leave aside any shyness, or whether you would have to talk with them.)

2. After fifteen minutes, everyone in the corner you have chosen leaves for another party across town except you. Of the groups *that still remain* now, which corner or group would you be drawn to the most?

3. After fifteen minutes, this group too leaves for another party, except you. Of the corners and groups which remain now, which one would you most enjoy being with?

SCORING AND INTERPRETATION

Each of the groups of people in "The Party" represent one of six personality/interest themes. The first step in interpreting your selections is an examination of the traits you have ranked one, two, and three, and how they define (at least in a general fashion) the skills that you most enjoy using.

Look at the letters listed with each party group and their corresponding descriptions below. Think about how much you would or would not enjoy working in the types of situations discussed and how the characteristics mentioned relate to your own personality.

As a further note, these themes can be combined to produce several hundred job personality types, each of which has something different to say about the match between an individual and an occupation. For example, a person who is primarily "realistic" (R) might also be "artistic" (A) and "enterprising" (E) and would probably find a job doing public relations layouts for the Forestry Service satisfying. Consider your examination of these areas, here, as a good first step in further vocational self-understanding.

R = Realistic. People high on the realistic theme tend to enjoy creating things with their hands and working with tools and objects rather than people and ideas. Such people tend to be rugged and practical, enjoying work outdoors. Examples of occupations that are primarily realistic in nature are those in construction, forestry, agriculture, and skilled crafts.

I = Investigative. Occupations high in investigative characteristics tend to focus on scientific activities. People high on this theme would often rather work alone than with other people and are usually seen as idea-oriented and creative in scientific areas such as research. Some specific investigative jobs are biologist, research psychologist, mathematician, technical writer, and computer programmer.

A = Artistic. People who score high on the artistic theme are artistically inclined, and usually describe themselves as independent, creative, and unconventional. They enjoy situations that allow them freedom to be original and are usually dissatisfied if they are forced to follow many rules and procedures. Some primarily artistic jobs include artist, musician, photographer, reporter, and interior decorator.

S = Social. People high on the social theme are usually seen by others as sociable, popular, and responsible. They are often interested in the problems and concerns of others, and tend to feel that things will generally work out for the best. Jobs that involve these personality aspects include social worker, guidance counselor, minister, nurse, and recreational leader.

E = Enterprising. Occupations that are primarily enterprising in nature usually involve sales or other situations where the person is in a position of leading or convincing others. People high on this theme are often seen as enthusiastic, dominant, and impatient. They like to be involved in jobs such as retail merchandising, real estate sales, law, television production, and political campaigning.

C = Conventional. High conventional people tend to prefer jobs where they are given firm structure and know exactly what is expected of them. People who rank high on this theme often describe themselves as conscientious, efficient, and calm. They enjoy words and numbers and systematic jobs such as bookkeeper, bank teller, accountant, secretary, and dental assistant.

ABOUT THE PARTY

We are attracted to people with the same interests and skills that we have. This truism was researched and put into vocational testing practice by psychologist John Holland. Dr. Holland found that in our culture most people can be categorized in terms of six types or themes: realistic, investigative, artistic, social, enterprising, and conventional. These characteristics are such that each individual's personality can be described by one or a combination of these types. Dr. Holland found that occupational environments had "personalities" as well, and could also be categorized by using these six themes. Investigating the relationship between the individual's personality and that of the job, Dr. Holland found that people search for job environments that will let them maximize the use of their skills, abilities, and values, while avoiding distasteful duties and responsibilities. The resulting interaction between the individual and the job's characteristics affects important concerns such as job performance, satisfaction, and stability. As Dr. Holland wrote, "The formulation for the types grew out of my experience as a vocational counselor and clinician, and out of my construction of a personality inventory from interest material."

The exercise that we have included here, "The Party," is the product of work by Richard Bolles, author of several popular books on job hunting and career change. He has developed a format for Dr. Holland's six themes that allows you to select and rank groups of people who are interesting to you. The basic idea is that your selections will, in a general way, relate to your social and vocational interests, as well as provide you with information about your own likes and dislikes.

The most significant use of Dr. Holland's themes in vocational testing is their role in the Strong-Campbell Interest Inventory (SCII), one of the best vocational tests available today. The SCII presents 325 items concerning specific occupations, school subjects, activities, amusements, types of people, and personal characteristics. The person taking the SCII responds by indicating "like," "indifferent," or "dislike" to each item, or by expressing a preference between two activities. The SCII is easy to take but very complex to score, and must be done by computer. The illustration below is of a page used to report SCII results. You will note how the test is divided—into sections R, I, A, S, E, C—which relate specific occupation and interest areas to Dr. Holland's six themes. Because of its complex nature, the SCII can only be taken through counseling centers, mental health clinics, or private practitioners, but it provides excellent information about the match between an individual's interests and the characteristics of a large number of occupations.

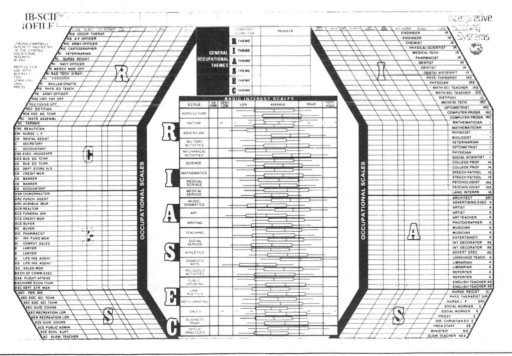

The results of the Strong-Campbell Interest Inventory are filled out by computer on forms similar to the one above. Reprinted from *Strong-Campbell Interest Inventory,* Form T325 of the *Strong Vocational Interest Blank,* by Edward K. Strong and David P. Campbell, with the permission of the publishers, Stanford University Press © 1974 by the Board of Trustees of the Leland Stanford Junior University.

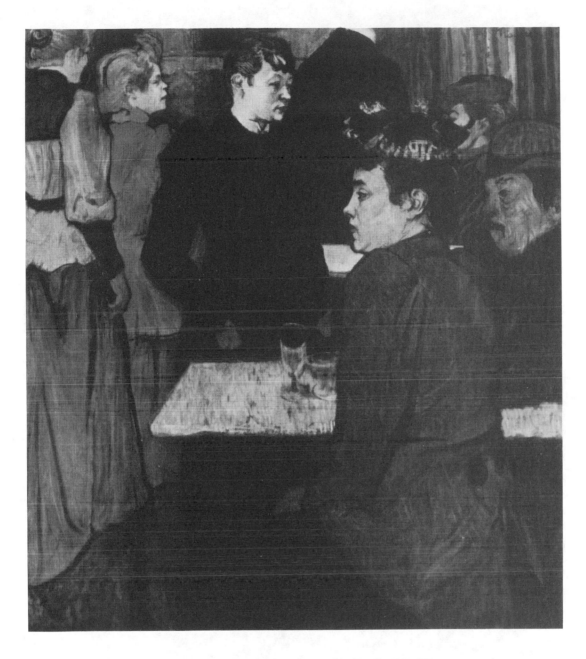

CHAPTER EIGHT

Interpersonal Relationships

*T*he most challenging of the psychological problems we face today are problems in interpersonal relationships. As individuals, each of us has particular talents, handicaps, and viewpoints that directly affect our interpersonal contacts. How we handle the relationships between our "selves" and others determines whether we will be happy and successful in life.

For the individual, the most acute block on the road to satisfactory interpersonal relationships is the inability to step outside the self and see it as others see it. We may be unhappy with our interpersonal relationships but find ourselves unable to attain our goals because of behavior we cannot perceive. To further complicate matters, we must all see ourselves and are identified by others in relation to some group, be it social, political, professional, racial, or religious. Thus it becomes even more difficult to separate our "selves" from our social habits and conditioning.

In order to live and work together on a day-to-day basis, we are often encouraged to build a shell around our feelings and thoughts, thus acting as others want us to—or at least as we think they do. This can become a social guessing game with interpersonal problems as the unwelcome prize. Those who have become aware of these problems and are concerned with their interpersonal relationships have helped give energy to the growth of psychotherapeutic methods such as assertiveness training, relaxation therapy, and encounter sessions that help improve social skills.

The most important tool in learning to communicate and in improving interpersonal relationships is accurate self-knowledge. The trick lies in finding a way to hold a mirror up to your personality and observe it in action. One way to look objectively at your personality is to select a single dimension of behavior—such as assertiveness, peer relations, or social avoidance—and use a written test to measure your strengths and concerns in that area. If, for example, you learn that your level of social satisfaction is hampered by your degree of assertiveness, you can work in that area toward overcoming the problem.

One way that these tests function is as a focusing device, a means of drawing attention to areas of strength, concern, or imbalance. This by no means implies that any test can produce a workable equation for successful human relations. The test merely gives you information about yourself and the way you relate to others. It is in your best interest to make your relationships work . . . and every bit of information can help.

Acceptance of Others Scale

by William F. Fey

Below you will find 20 statements that deal with some of your feelings and attitudes about other people. Read each statement carefully and decide how true you feel the statement to be. Using the accompanying scale in the next column, place the number which indicates your feelings about that statement in the space provided on the answer sheet. Pay attention to your first response and try not to spend too long on any one statement. After taking the test, turn the page to find your score.

1 = **Almost always true**

2 = **Usually true**

3 = **True half of the time**

4 = **Only occasionally true**

5 = **Very rarely true**

_____ 1. People are too easily led.

_____ 2. I like people I get to know.

_____ 3. People these days have pretty low moral standards.

_____ 4. Most people are pretty smug about themselves, never really facing their bad points.

_____ 5. I can be comfortable with nearly all kinds of people.

_____ 6. All people can talk about these days, it seems, is movies, TV, and foolishness like that.

_____ 7. People get ahead by using "pull," and not because of what they know.

_____ 8. Once you start doing favors for people, they'll just walk all over you.

_____ 9. People are too self-centered.

_____ 10. People are always dissatisfied and hunting for something new.

_____ 11. With many people you don't know how you stand.

_____ 12. You've probably got to hurt someone if you're going to make something out of yourself.

_____ 13. People really need a strong, smart leader.

_____ 14. I enjoy myself most when I am alone, away from people.

_____ 15. I wish people would be more honest with me.

_____ 16. I enjoy going with a crowd.

_____ 17. In my experience, people are pretty stubborn and unreasonable.

_____ 18. I can enjoy being with people whose values are very different from mine.

_____ 19. Everybody tries to be nice.

_____ 20. The average person is not very well satisfied with himself.

William F. Fey, "Acceptance by others and its relation to acceptance of self and others: A revaluation," *Journal of Abnormal and Social Psychology,* 1955, *30,* 274–276. Copyright 1955 by the American Psychological Association. Reprinted by permission.

SCORING KEY

	A	B
1.	_____	
2. Reverse		_____
3.	_____	
4.	_____	
5. Reverse		_____
6.	_____	
7.	_____	
8.	_____	
9.	_____	
10.	_____	
11.	_____	
12.	_____	
13.	_____	
14.	_____	
15.	_____	
16. Reverse		_____
17.	_____	
18. Reverse		_____
19. Reverse		_____
20.	_____	

FOLD BACK TO SCORE

SCORING THE SCALE

To find your score, fold this page back along the dotted line, then transfer your answers for items 1, 3, 4, 6 etc. into column A. Next, for items 2, 5, 16, 18, and 19 *reverse the score* as shown below and enter in column B.

In column B, an answer of

1 earns 5 points

2 earns 4 points

3 earns 3 points

4 earns 2 points

5 earns 1 point

To find your final score, add together the total points in both columns and enter in the box below.

TOTAL SCORE

INTERPRETING YOUR SCORE

Dr. Fey's research during the development of this scale showed that the average test score was 75. He found that two out of three people in his test development group scored between 66 and 84. That means that approximately 20 percent scored 65 or less and approximately 20 percent scored above 84.

Low Scorers (0–65)—If you scored in the low range, you're scoring similar to people who often report being intolerant of others. Perhaps you feel this way because you've been "stung" by others; things have happened to you which have caused you to lose faith in people and become disillusioned about them. This lack of tolerance and acceptance of others may reflect, as Dr. Fey discusses, a lack of self-acceptance. Other tests available to you in *The Mind Test* may help you sort out that part of your personality. However it's caused, a lack of acceptance of others can make for an empty life. That kind of a problem, if it does indeed exist for you, calls for continued self-examination.

Medium Scorers (66–84)—If you scored around the average for the test, your life is likely to be a mix of caution and acceptance of others. If you've been hurt by others, it may have resulted in a cautious approach to certain people or certain types of people. But even with caution, you probably have close friends and the desire for close relationships. You are just likely to be choosier than high scorers.

High Scorers (85–100)—High scorers are reported to be a pretty happy group. They generally accept others, feel accepted by others, and tend to be accepted by others. Now, you may have scored in this range yet feel like saying, "But others *don't* seem to accept me." Quite possible, according to Dr. Fey's research. He points out that people who are high both in self-acceptance and acceptance of others—"the prototypic well-adjusted person"—may not be well liked. He writes, "Perhaps the average person cannot identify easily with the overt paragon of emotional good health. Such a person may not appear to 'need' friendship. . . . It may be that his very psychological robustness is resented." Even if this predicament shows itself for you, you no doubt have the self-confidence and support from *meaningful* relationships to weather any rocky times.

ABOUT THE SCALE

One of the most popular of modern psychologists, Dr. Carl Rogers, has based his approach to understanding human concerns on those problems that stem from our difficulties in accepting ourselves the way we are. Other psychologists have taken his interest in self-acceptance and studied the relationship between how well we accept ourselves and how well we are able to accept others.

Dr. William Fey developed the Acceptance of Others Scale for this specific purpose. His review of available research suggested that psychologists need to study acceptance of self and acceptance of others as a personality combination. His work found that attitudes of self-acceptance and acceptance of others tended to go hand in hand for most people. Thus how you answer the questions on a test such as this one may reflect, to some degree, how you feel about yourself. It is also interesting to note that psychologists feel that whether or not you are accepted by others is partially determined by this interrelationship between your attitudes toward yourself and your feelings toward others. According to Dr. Fey, "It is quite possible that the genuinely self-accepting person truly accepts others, that he does not threaten them and is rewarded in turn by their acceptance."

Social Interest Scale

by James E. Crandall

Below are a number of pairs of personal characteristics or traits. For each pair, underline the trait which you value more highly. In making each choice, ask yourself which of the traits in that pair you would rather possess as one of your own characteristics. For example, the first pair is "imaginative—rational." If you had to make a choice, which would you rather be? Draw a line under your choice in each of the pairs.

Some of the traits will appear twice, but always in combination with a different other trait. No pairs will be repeated.

"I would rather be . . ."

imaginative	rational
helpful	quick-witted
neat	sympathetic
level-headed	efficient
intelligent	considerate
self-reliant	ambitious
respectful	original
creative	sensible
generous	individualistic
responsible	original
capable	tolerant
trustworthy	wise
neat	logical
forgiving	gentle
efficient	respectful
practical	self-confident
capable	independent
alert	cooperative
imaginative	helpful
realistic	moral
considerate	wise
sympathetic	individualistic
ambitious	patient
reasonable	quick-witted

ABOUT THE SCALE

In 1911, Alfred Adler, originally a disciple of Sigmund Freud, broke from Freudian psychology to develop his own views on personality, pathology, and therapy. Adler's main criticism of Freud's work was its lack of concern for the social, interpersonal life of the individual. This concept of social interest remains, today, as the cardinal characteristic of Adler's theories.

Adler defined social interest in terms of an "interest in the interests of mankind." He saw it as a positive attitude toward others, concern for their welfare, and empathetic and sympathetic understanding of their needs. Perhaps what social interest is *not* can be illustrated by this brief story:

You're walking home from shopping. Suddenly you see a man in front of you hit by a car and badly hurt. You rush to the scene of the accident and stop next to a man looking down at the injured pedestrian.

He turns to you and says, "It's been a terrible day for Phil Wilson."

"Is that the poor guy who's been hurt?" you ask.

"No," the bystander replies, "I'm Phil Wilson."

Psychologist James Crandall noted in 1975, after his review of the theoretical work in the area of social interest, ". . . it was surprising to find that there apparently has been no attempt to develop a standardized measure of the concept." The Social Interest Scale reflects his work to develop just such a measure. You'll find that this test is unlike many of the others in *The Mind Test*. Rather than "yes-no" or "true-false" questions, the Social Interest Scale asks you to choose which of two personal traits you value more highly. This choice forces you to think about your own interests and about what is important to you as you relate to other people. Such an approach is consistent with the concepts developed by Alfred Adler. It allows you to determine which traits *you* value rather than responding on the basis of what you think others (society) would like you to say.

SCORING THE SCALE

Your score on the Social Interest Scale is the number of times that the trait you've underlined matches the one *italicized* in the key. Note that the key contains only 15 italicized traits. Nine of the pairs are called "buffer" pairs and are used to separate the pairs which Dr. Crandall uses to measure social interest. In effect, the buffer pairs make what the test is really trying to measure a little less obvious. To find your score, fold this page back on the dotted line and compare your answers to those on the Scoring Key. Give yourself one point for each matching *italicized* word.

SCORING KEY

		Match
imaginative	rational	
helpful	quick-witted	_____
neat	*sympathetic*	_____
level-headed	efficient	
intelligent	*considerate*	_____
self-reliant	ambitious	
respectful	original	_____
creative	sensible	
generous	individualistic	_____
responsible	original	
capable	*tolerant*	_____
trustworthy	wise	_____
neat	logical	
forgiving	gentle	_____
efficient	*respectful*	_____
practical	self-confident	
capable	independent	
alert	*cooperative*	_____
imaginative	*helpful*	_____
realistic	*moral*	_____
considerate	wise	_____
sympathetic	individualistic	_____
ambitious	*patient*	_____
reasonable	quick-witted	

TOTAL SCORE

FOLD BACK TO SCORE

INTERPRETING YOUR SCORE

Low Scorers (0–6)—People who score in this range are frequently seen by others as showing little interest, liking, or concern for other people. If you are a low scorer, values such as pleasure and excitement in life are probably important to you. There may be times when your emphasis on personal pleasure makes it hard for you to show concern for others. Of course, showing concern and feeling concern may not be the same for you. It is possible that some of your behavior that others may see as self-centered is not intended to express the lack of social interest that it does. Your interpersonal relationships could improve if others had a better understanding of your interest in them.

Medium Scorers (7–11)—Scorers in this range are seen by others as neither highly concerned about the welfare of mankind nor as extremely self-centered. You may actually be quite concerned about the welfare of others. Your social interest, however, may be focused on specific people, sometimes causing others to feel that you're not particularly concerned about the general human condition. If you are comfortable with how and toward whom you express your social interest, then any negative comments from others will not (and probably should not) concern you.

High Scorers (11–15)—If you scored in this range, other people probably see you as genuinely concerned about humanitarian issues in your community. You emphasize in your dealings with others their concerns and feelings and are probably quick to help someone in need. High scorers generally value peace, equality, and family security more than they value personal pleasure or an exciting life. You most likely concern yourself with your loved ones and those relationships serve as a source of satisfaction for you. In addition, consistent with Adler's theories, high social interest people seem to be satisfied with life in general and report less depression and unhappiness than those who score low on this scale.

Index of Peer Relations

by Walter W. Hudson

This questionnaire is designed to measure the way you feel about the people you work, play, or associate with most of the time, your peer group. It is not a test so there are no right or wrong answers. Answer each item below as carefully and as accurately as you can by placing a number beside each one as follows:

1 = *Rarely or none of the time*
2 = *A little of the time*
3 = *Some of the time*
4 = *A good part of the time*
5 = *Most or all of the time*

_____ 1. I get along very well with my peers.

_____ 2. My peers act like they don't care about me.

_____ 3. My peers treat me badly.

_____ 4. My peers really seem to respect me.

_____ 5. I don't feel like I am "part of the group."

_____ 6. My peers are a bunch of snobs.

_____ 7. My peers really understand me.

_____ 8. My peers seem to like me very much.

_____ 9. I really feel "left out" of my peer group.

_____ 10. I hate my present peer group.

_____ 11. My peers seem to like having me around.

_____ 12. I really like my present peer group.

_____ 13. I really feel like I am disliked by my peers.

_____ 14. I wish I had a different peer group.

_____ 15. My peers are very nice to me.

_____ 16. My peers seem to look up to me.

_____ 17. My peers think I am important to them.

_____ 18. My peers are a real source of pleasure to me.

_____ 19. My peers don't seem to even notice me.

_____ 20. I wish I were not part of this peer group.

_____ 21. My peers regard my ideas and opinions very highly.

_____ 22. I feel like I am an important member of my peer group.

_____ 23. I can't stand to be around my peer group.

_____ 24. My peers seem to look down on me.

_____ 25. My peers really do not interest me.

To find your total score, fold this page forward along the dotted line to compare your answers with those on the Scoring Key.

First, transfer your answers into the boxes in column A for items 2, 3, 5, 6, etc. Next, in column B, reverse the numerical value of your answers for items 1, 4, 7, 8, etc. For example:

In column B an answer of

1 earns 5 points

2 earns 4 points

3 earns 3 points

4 earns 2 points

5 earns 1 point

To find your total score, add together the total points in column A and the total points in column B. From this sum, subtract 25 points. The result is your final score.

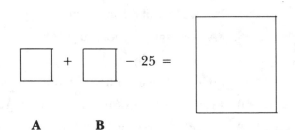

A   B

TOTAL
SCORE

SCORING KEY

	A	B
1.	Reverse	_____
2.	_____	
3.	_____	
4.	Reverse	_____
5.	_____	
6.	_____	
7.	Reverse	_____
8.	Reverse	_____
9.	_____	
10.	_____	
11.	Reverse	_____
12.	Reverse	_____
13.	_____	
14.	_____	
15.	Reverse	_____
16.	Reverse	_____
17.	Reverse	_____
18.	Reverse	_____
19.	_____	
20.	_____	
21.	Reverse	_____
22.	Reverse	_____
23.	_____	
24.	_____	
25.	_____	

FOLD BACK TO SCORE

INTERPRETING YOUR SCORE

Below Average Scorers (0–30)—If you scored in this range, you've scored similar to people who are comfortable with their present peer group; a *low* score on this test is a *high* level of satisfaction. Your score suggests that your peer situation provides you with rewards for your ideas and for being who you are as a person. In addition, the people you consider part of your peer group are likely to serve as sources of emotional support for you when times get rough. In fact, if you scored in the higher part of this range (close to 30), a potential problem for you could be that you don't rely on your peers as much as you would find helpful. You may want to think about that and give those people a try when you need them.

Above Average Scorers (31–100)—People who score in this range often report significant problems in relating to their peer group. If this statement fits your present feelings and life situation, it's important for you to think about what it is about you or your peer group that may be causing the problem. For example, your problem could relate to a sheer lack of people around you who can provide emotional support when you need it. Or the problem may be caused by an unpleasant job situation that forces you into a less desirable work peer group. (See Chapter 7 for further examination of vocation.) You may need work in some interpersonal area, such as social skills, in order for you to feel more comfortable in giving and getting from your peer group. Other tests in this book may help point out some of those areas to you. If your peer group situation is a very serious problem for you, combining this kind of self-understanding with professional help will prove valuable.

ABOUT THE INDEX

Each of us has a specific group of people who are important to us. They may be people in the neighborhood, co-workers from our job, or a circle of friends. No matter who they are, our peer group serves a very important function for each of us. The people in this group provide us with guidelines for our behavior, social contacts which keep life interesting, and rewards which help us feel good about ourselves. In fact, many psychological theories of personality development emphasize the role of our peer groups in affecting how we develop as social beings. And with our social development comes the related development of our personal attitudes and emotional strengths.

In his position as a professor of social work, Dr. Walter Hudson became interested in evaluating the impact of peer group satisfaction on the emotional functioning of those in the group. As part of the development of a "clinical measurement package" for use in social work, Dr. Hudson designed the Index of Peer Relations. The test presents a series of straightforward statements which ask you about your feelings toward those people you include in your own peer group. You'll find other tests developed by Dr. Hudson as part of his "package" in other chapters of *The Mind Test*.

Assertion Questionnaire

by Peter Lewinsohn

Go over the list of questions twice.

First, *rate each item using the "Frequency Scale" in the next column. Rate each on how often it has occurred during the past month.*

Second, *rate how comfortable you were when each situation happened, or how comfortable you would be if it were to happen. For this rating, use the "Comfort Scale."*

As Dr. Lewinsohn points out, there are no right or wrong answers to the items on this questionnaire. As with all the tests in **The Mind Test,** *its primary purpose is to provide you with information about yourself.*

FREQUENCY SCALE

Indicate how often each of these events occurred by marking the Frequency Column, using the following scale:

*1 = This has **not** happened in the past 30 days*

*2 = This has happened a **few times** (1 to 6 times) in the past 30 days*

*3 = This has happened **often** (7 times or more) in the past 30 days*

COMFORT SCALE

Indicate how you feel about each of these events by marking the Comfort Column, using the following scale:

*1 = I felt **very uncomfortable or upset** when this happened*

*2 = I felt **somewhat uncomfortable or upset** when this happened*

*3 = I felt **neutral** when this happened (neither comfortable nor uncomfortable; neither good nor upset)*

*4 = I felt **fairly comfortable or good** when this happened*

*5 = I felt **very comfortable or good** when this happened*

Important: If an event has not happened during the past month, then rate it according to how you think you would feel if it happened. If an event happened more than once in the past month, rate roughly how you felt about it on the average.

	Frequency	Comfort
1. Turning down a person's request to borrow my car	____	____
2. Asking a favor of someone	____	____
3. Resisting sales pressure	____	____
4. Admitting fear and requesting consideration	____	____
5. Telling a person I am intimately involved with that he/she has said or done something that bothers me	____	____
6. Admitting ignorance in an area being discussed	____	____
7. Turning down a friend's request to borrow money	____	____
8. Turning off a talkative friend	____	____
9. Asking for constructive criticism	____	____
10. Asking for clarification when I am confused about what someone has said	____	____
11. Asking whether I have offended someone	____	____
12. Telling a person of the opposite sex that I like him/her	____	____
13. Telling a person of the same sex that I like him/her	____	____
14. Requesting expected service when it hasn't been offered (e.g., in a restaurant)	____	____
15. Discussing openly with a person his/her criticism of my behavior	____	____
16. Returning defective items (e.g., at a store or restaurant)	____	____
17. Expressing an opinion that differs from that of a person I am talking with	____	____
18. Resisting sexual overtures when I am not interested	____	____
19. Telling someone how I feel if he/she has done something that is unfair to me	____	____
20. Turning down a social invitation from someone I don't particularly like	____	____
21. Resisting pressure to drink	____	____
22. Resisting an unfair demand from a person who is important to me	____	____
23. Requesting the return of borrowed items	____	____
24. Telling a friend or co-worker when he/she says or does something that bothers me	____	____
25. Asking a person who is annoying me in a public situation to stop (e.g., smoking on a bus)	____	____
26. Criticizing a friend	____	____
27. Criticizing my spouse	____	____
28. Asking someone for help or advice	____	____
29. Expressing my love to someone	____	____
30. Asking to borrow something	____	____
31. Giving my opinion when a group is discussing an important matter	____	____
32. Taking a definite stand on a controversial issue	____	____
33. When two friends are arguing, supporting the one I agree with	____	____
34. Expressing my opinion to someone I don't know very well	____	____
35. Interrupting someone to ask him/her to repeat something I didn't hear clearly	____	____
36. Contradicting someone when I think I might hurt him/her by doing so	____	____
37. Telling someone that he/she has disappointed me or let me down	____	____
38. Asking someone to leave me alone	____	____
39. Telling a friend or co-worker that he/she has done a good job	____	____
40. Telling someone he/she has made a good point in a discussion	____	____
41. Telling someone I have enjoyed talking with him/her	____	____
42. Complimenting someone on his/her skill or creativity.	____	____

SCORING THE QUESTIONNAIRE

To find your Assertion Frequency score, add up the numbers you've placed in the "frequency" column. Enter that number in the appropriate box. To compute your Assertion Comfort score, add up the numbers you've placed in that column next to the questions. Place your Comfort score in the appropriate box.

ASSERTION FREQUENCY SCORE

ASSERTION COMFORT SCORE

INTERPRETING YOUR SCORE

Most people score within the following ranges:

Assertion Frequency: 61–81
Assertion Comfort: 102–137

This means that the typical individual has had most of the listed situations occur at least a few times during the past month. Further, this typical person probably feels at least fairly comfortable with being assertive in several of the situations and neutral to somewhat uncomfortable in some others. If you scored higher than these average scores, you probably know when you're being appropriately assertive (and would very likely write us a letter telling us that we're wrong if we said anything different about you).

If you scored near the bottom of the average ranges, it may just have been an unusually nonassertive month for you. Next month may find you acting (and scoring) more assertively, particularly now that you're thinking about it.

If you scored way below the average ranges, however, lack of assertiveness and discomfort with being assertive may be a real problem and major concern for you. No doubt you spend a lot of time wishing you could tell people how you feel; in fact, you may feel at times like the guy who gets sand kicked into his face at the beach and just lies there and takes it. Unfortunately, no comic-book strength gimmick is going to help you become more assertive. One step, only a first one of several, is taking this test, reading this discussion, and thinking about whether lack of assertiveness is a problem for you. The next step is to move a little closer to doing something about the problem if it indeed does exist for you. A trusted friend may be able to serve as a good listener and help direct you toward more assertive behavior. Some counseling programs dealing with assertiveness training may now be worth the emotional risk. It's not going to be easy. You're going to have to *be* more assertive in order to work on becoming more assertive. Such a bind is a major reason why professional help in assertiveness training is most often the best way to go.

ABOUT THE QUESTIONNAIRE

Assertion is an area of social skill behavior that often causes people difficulty in dealing with others. Assertiveness involves defending ourselves and expressing what we are thinking and feeling. To some, the idea of assertiveness is very negative. They consider assertiveness the same as being obnoxious and demanding, without regard to the feelings of others. Psychologists, however, see assertiveness in a much broader and more positive way, as a healthy means of open expression. Certainly some of the things that a person may express openly can be seen as negative, but being assertive also means being able to share the positive parts of ourselves, our hopes and fears, our affection and concern for others. In this light, assertiveness becomes a very important part of a close, two-way relationship wherein each person trusts the other to be honest and open.

Psychologist Dr. Peter Lewinsohn also sees assertiveness on a very practical level. Dr. Lewinsohn states in his book *Control Your Depression,*

It [assertiveness] helps avoid or prevent aversive encounters with others; no one can take advantage of someone who is properly assertive. Second, those who are appropriately assertive are likely to get more positive feelings from other people; they express more positive feelings and they receive them in return. . . . Finally, those who are more appropriately assertive feel better understood by others. . . . People can't know how you feel and show their caring unless you take the first step of expressing your own thoughts and feelings.

The Assertion Questionnaire we've included here was developed by Dr. Lewinsohn along with his colleagues Drs. Munoz, Youngren, and Zeiss as part of their work relating depression to a person's lack of specific social skills, such as assertiveness. The questions on the scale measure both how assertive you are and how comfortable you are with your assertiveness in certain situations.

APPENDICES

SELECTING A THERAPIST

Most people know very little about the mental health system when they start looking for help. Often people find a therapist by accident and do not feel comfortable that the match between them and the therapist is the best possible.

One way to find a therapist is through people you know who are willing to be involved in your search for information. They may be familiar with specific agencies or individual practitioners who work well with the kinds of problems you are experiencing. Usually the most helpful of this type of information can come from your family, friends, physicians, and clergy. They may be able to give you a specific name or at least refer you to someone who can answer your questions for you. Once you have a name or two in hand, your telephone can provide the next step—that of gaining firsthand information about the agency or practitioner. Since you are placing yourself in the role of consumer, you will need specific information about your therapist *before* you make a choice. The National Directory of Mental Health lists these questions as ones you may want to ask over the telephone:

> Where did the therapist receive his or her training and in which mental health field? What is the therapist's psychological point of view? What is the cost or price range (if fees are negotiable) of the therapist's services? What are the possibilities for arranging a face-to-face evaluative interview?

If you are contacting a mental health clinic, you may be told that before being assigned a specific therapist, you will need to come in for an initial interview. Even in this situation, you can ask questions similar to the above about the agency and its service staff.

The initial interview will allow you to discuss the nature of your problems or concerns and your goals for treatment. The primary question that you will be asked is, "What has happened to bring you here at this specific time?" In addition, you and the therapist will need to know some of each other's values, beliefs, and life-style in order to be certain that there are no major conflicts which would interfere with your working together. Most consumer guides (and practitioners, as well) encourage you to be assertive in evaluating and choosing a therapist. This will not be as easy as it may sound, however. Since many of the problems which cause people to seek therapy also involve feelings of depression and insecurity, it is often difficult to be assertive and spend a lot of energy in this evaluation process. Keep in mind that if the initial meeting with your potential therapist *increases* your bad feelings, then you may not be buying what is best for you psychologically. If you feel that this arrangement will not work out, either request assignment to a different therapist or continue your own search.

INFORMATION ABOUT AVAILABLE SERVICES

Within the mental health field, there is a wide range of practitioners and, in each area, varying levels of expertise. Where you will want to go for help will depend on factors in addition to the nature of your concerns, such as your economic resources, age, sex, and educational background. In general, professional help is available through community mental health clinics, private mental health clinics, and practitioners in private practice. Within the group of practitioners offering private therapy, there are several different types of professionals, such as psychologists, psychiatrists, counselors, and social workers, to name a few. Most professional groups have established criteria for competency recognition within that field. Such information should be provided readily by any potential therapist or agency.

Helpful Addresses for Psychological Information *

American Psychological Association
1200 Seventeenth Street, NW
Washington, D.C. 20036

Canadian Psychological Association
Suite 46, 1390 Sherbrooke Street West
Montreal 109, Quebec, Canada

*In addition, most of these national organizations have state, regional, or provincial associations which will be listed in your local telephone book.

American Psychiatric Association
1700 Eighteenth Street NW
Washington, D.C. 20009

Canadian Psychiatric Association
Suite 103, 225 Lisgar Street
Ottawa, Ontario K2P 0C6, Canada

National Association for Mental Health
1800 North Kent Street
Rosslyn, VA 22209

Canadian Mental Health Association
52 St. Clair Avenue East
Toronto, Ontario, Canada

National Association of Social Work
1425 H Street NW, Suite 600
Washington, D.C. 20005

National Register of Health Service Providers
in Psychology
1200 Seventeenth Street NW
Washington, D.C. 20036

American Group Psychotherapy Association
1865 Broadway, 12th Floor
New York, NY 10023

Public Citizen's Health Research Group/
Ralph Nader
2000 P Street, NW
Washington, D.C. 20005

National Information Numbers

National Clearinghouse for Mental Health Information: (301) 443-4514
National Clearinghouse for Drug Abuse Information: (301) 443-6500
National Clearinghouse for Alcohol Information: (301) 468-2600
Operation Venus (VD Information): (800) 523-1885
Cancer Information Service: (800) 628-6694
Veterans Administration Information Service: (202) 389-2443

Attitudes Toward Seeking Professional Psychological Help Scale

by Edward H. Fischer
and John L. Turner

On the next page are a number of statements pertaining to psychology and mental health issues. Read each statement carefully and indicate your agreement, possible disagreement, or disagreement using the scale below. Please express your frank opinion in responding to each statement, answering as you honestly feel or believe.

0 = Disagreement
1 = Probable Disagreement
2 = Probable Agreement
3 = Agreement

Fischer, E. H., and Turner, J. L. "Orientations to seeking professional help: Development and research utility of an attitude scale." *Journal of Consulting and Clinical Psychology,* 1970, *35,* 82–83. Copyright 1970 by the American Psychological Association. Reprinted by permission.

1. Although there are clinics for people with mental troubles, I would not have much faith in them.

2. If a good friend asked my advice about a mental health problem, I might recommend that he see a psychiatrist.

3. I would feel uneasy going to a psychiatrist because of what some people would think.

4. A person with a strong character can get over mental conflicts by himself, and would have little need of a psychiatrist.

5. There are times when I have felt completely lost and would have welcomed professional advice for a personal or emotional problem.

6. Considering the time and expense involved in psychotherapy, it would have doubtful value for a person like me.

7. I would willingly confide intimate matters to an appropriate person if I thought it might help me or a member of my family.

8. I would rather live with certain mental conflicts than go through the ordeal of getting psychiatric treatment.

9. Emotional difficulties, like many things, tend to work out by themselves.

10. There are certain problems that should not be discussed outside of one's immediate family.

11. A person with a serious emotional disturbance would probably feel most secure in a good mental hospital.

12. If I believed I was having a mental breakdown, my first inclination would be to get professional attention.

13. Keeping one's mind on a job is a good solution for avoiding personal worries and concerns.

14. Having been a psychiatric patient is a blot on a person's life.

15. I would rather be advised by a close friend than by a psychologist, even for an emotional problem.

16. A person with an emotional problem is not likely to solve it alone; he *is* likely to solve it with professional help.

17. I resent a person—professionally trained or not—who wants to know about my personal difficulties.

18. I would want to get psychiatric attention if I was worried or upset for a long period of time.

19. The idea of talking about problems with a psychologist strikes me as a poor way to get rid of emotional conflicts.

20. Having been mentally ill carries with it a burden of shame.

21. There are experiences in my life I would not discuss with anyone.

22. It is probably best not to know *everything* about oneself.

23. If I were experiencing a serious emotional crisis at this point in my life, I would be confident that I could find relief in psychotherapy.

24. There is something admirable in the attitude of a person who is willing to cope with his conflicts and fears *without* resorting to professional help.

25. At some future time I might want to have psychological counseling.

26. A person should work out his own problems; getting psychological counseling would be a last resort.

27. Had I received treatment in a mental hospital, I would not feel that it had to be "covered up."

28. If I thought I needed psychiatric help, I would get it no matter who knew about it.

29. It is difficult to talk about personal affairs with highly educated people such as doctors, teachers, and clergymen.

_____ 1.
_____ 2.
_____ 3.
_____ 4.
_____ 5.
_____ 6.
_____ 7.
_____ 8.
_____ 9.
_____ 10.
_____ 11.
_____ 12.
_____ 13.
_____ 14.
_____ 15.
_____ 16.
_____ 17.
_____ 18.
_____ 19.
_____ 20.
_____ 21.
_____ 22.
_____ 23.
_____ 24.
_____ 25.
_____ 26.
_____ 27.
_____ 28.
_____ 29.

ABOUT THE SCALE

One of the most difficult decisions confronting an individual who is in a state of emotional pain is the major step in seeking professional help—that of making the initial therapy contact. Although we live in what some consider enlightened times, our society still encourages people to be independent and autonomous, even during periods of emotional distress. Many people find that making the decision to seek psychological help produces more additional stress than they are willing to accept. Thus they try to live with their problems rather than to reduce or eliminate them through the most effective means available to them.

Psychologists Edward Fischer and John Turner saw the need for a scale that would assess this reluctance (or positive orientation) to seek professional help. Their first step was to develop an understanding of the reasons involved in a reluctance for treatment. They wrote, "One person may view the decision to get professional help as a sign of personal weakness, indicative of failure; for him the move to get professional help represents a last-ditch desperate action spurred by a psychologically intolerable situation." Yet they also noted that other individuals seek help willingly, genuinely expecting appreciable life changes.

There is no doubt as to the importance of attitude toward therapy in affecting therapy success. Anthropologist William Gladstone stated,

> Studies have shown that the most important preconditions for successful therapy are belief in the particular type of therapy undertaken and confidence and trust in the therapeutic practitioner. If you are to engage in successful therapy, you must believe that you are participating in a worthwhile activity and that your sacrifices of time and money will be repaid by the attainment of improved mental health.

Thus, the concepts being measured by the scale developed by Drs. Fischer and Turner reflect serious issues, not only in the seeking of help but in having that help be effective.

SCORING KEY

	A	B
1. Reverse		_____
2.	_____	
3. Reverse		_____
4. Reverse		_____
5.	_____	
6. Reverse		_____
7.	_____	
8. Reverse		_____
9. Reverse		_____
10. Reverse		_____
11.	_____	
12.	_____	
13. Reverse		_____
14. Reverse		_____
15. Reverse		_____
16.	_____	
17. Reverse		_____
18.	_____	
19. Reverse		_____
20. Reverse		_____
21. Reverse		_____
22. Reverse		_____
23.	_____	
24. Reverse		_____
25.	_____	
26. Reverse		_____
27.	_____	
28.	_____	
29. Reverse		_____

SCORING THE SCALE

To score the scale, fold this page back along the dotted line in order to line up your answers with the Scoring Key.

First, transfer your answers into the spaces in Column A for items 2, 5, 7, 11, etc.

Next, in column B, reverse the numerical value of your answers for items 1, 3, 4, 6, etc. For example:

In Column B, an answer of

0 earns 3 points

1 earns 2 points

2 earns 1 point

3 earns 0 points

To find your final score, add together the totals of Columns A and B and record them in the box below.

TOTAL SCORE

◄ FOLD BACK TO SCORE ◄

INTERPRETING YOUR SCORE

Low Scorers (29–49)—Low scorers on this scale are expressing a negative attitude toward seeking professional help for themselves or for their friends. This does not mean that you, if you scored in this range, are having problems or have any need for professional help. It indicates, rather, that if you *were* to be feeling high levels of stress, or depression, or anxiety for example, you would not be inclined to turn to a mental health professional for assistance. The test does not answer the question of why you feel this reluctance. Perhaps some possible stigma associated with therapy is a major concern for you, or perhaps you feel that seeking help is a sign of weakness. Spend some time examining your feelings and make an attempt to learn what exactly is involved in the therapy process. Such self-examination and information-gathering now, while your life is going well, may prove quite valuable if you or a friend are ever confronted with the need for professional help.

Medium Scorers (50–63)—Medium scorers are acknowledging that professional help can be useful but that they are somewhat unsure about their willingness to use it. As a medium scorer you may find it useful to get additional information regarding the therapy process. Such information may clarify what the therapy process is all about. Since you are expressing an overall willingness to consider therapy, the important aspect of your attitude is how confident you are that therapy would work if you were to need it. Use your friends, books, and professionals to provide you with answers to your questions and concerns about psychological treatment.

High Scorers (64–87)—High scorers are expressing a very positive attitude toward seeking and using professional help. In terms of related personality characteristics, the research by Drs. Fischer and Turner suggests that high scorers are also internally controlled people. That is, as a high scorer you are likely to see the control of your life resting in your own hands and believe that your own actions determine whether you feel good or bad, whether you experience failure or success. Seeking help when you feel you need it is one way to use that control to improve your life. Such a positive orientation toward seeking help strongly suggests that if you ever do need professional help, you will make use of it and that it is likely to be very effective.

THE MIND TEST

DIRECTIONS: Blacken in the boxes under T (True) or F (False) to show your response to each question.

Be careful to see that the number you mark is the same as the number of the question you are answering.

	T	F		T	F		T	F		T	F		T	F		T	F		T	F		T	F
1.	☐	☐	2.	☐	☐	3.	☐	☐	4.	☐	☐	5.	☐	☐	6.	☐	☐	7.	☐	☐	8.	☐	☐
9.	☐	☐	10.	☐	☐	11.	☐	☐	12.	☐	☐	13.	☐	☐	14.	☐	☐	15.	☐	☐	16.	☐	☐
17.	☐	☐	18.	☐	☐	19.	☐	☐	20.	☐	☐	21.	☐	☐	22.	☐	☐	23.	☐	☐	24.	☐	☐
25.	☐	☐	26.	☐	☐	27.	☐	☐	28.	☐	☐	29.	☐	☐	30.	☐	☐	31.	☐	☐	32.	☐	☐
33.	☐	☐	34.	☐	☐	35.	☐	☐	36.	☐	☐	37.	☐	☐	38.	☐	☐	39.	☐	☐	40.	☐	☐

	T	F		T	F		T	F		T	F		T	F		T	F		T	F		T	F
41.	☐	☐	42.	☐	☐	43.	☐	☐	44.	☐	☐	45.	☐	☐	46.	☐	☐	47.	☐	☐	48.	☐	☐
49.	☐	☐	50.	☐	☐	51.	☐	☐	52.	☐	☐	53.	☐	☐	54.	☐	☐	55.	☐	☐	56.	☐	☐
57.	☐	☐	58.	☐	☐	59.	☐	☐	60.	☐	☐	61.	☐	☐	62.	☐	☐	63.	☐	☐	64.	☐	☐
65.	☐	☐	66.	☐	☐	67.	☐	☐	68.	☐	☐	69.	☐	☐	70.	☐	☐	71.	☐	☐	72.	☐	☐
73.	☐	☐	74.	☐	☐	75.	☐	☐	76.	☐	☐	77.	☐	☐	78.	☐	☐	79.	☐	☐	80.	☐	☐

	T	F		T	F		T	F		T	F		T	F		T	F		T	F		T	F
81.	☐	☐	82.	☐	☐	83.	☐	☐	84.	☐	☐	85.	☐	☐	86.	☐	☐	87.	☐	☐	88.	☐	☐
89.	☐	☐	90.	☐	☐	91.	☐	☐	92.	☐	☐	93.	☐	☐	94.	☐	☐	95.	☐	☐	96.	☐	☐
97.	☐	☐	98.	☐	☐	99.	☐	☐	100.	☐	☐	101.	☐	☐	102.	☐	☐	103.	☐	☐	104.	☐	☐
105.	☐	☐	106.	☐	☐	107.	☐	☐	108.	☐	☐	109.	☐	☐	110.	☐	☐	111.	☐	☐	112.	☐	☐
113.	☐	☐	114.	☐	☐	115.	☐	☐	116.	☐	☐	117.	☐	☐	118.	☐	☐	119.	☐	☐	120.	☐	☐

THE MIND TEST

DIRECTIONS: Blacken in the boxes under T (True) or F (False) to show your response to each question.

Be careful to see that the number you mark is the same as the number of the question you are answering.

	T	F		T	F		T	F		T	F		T	F		T	F		T	F		T	F
1.	☐	☐	2.	☐	☐	3.	☐	☐	4.	☐	☐	5.	☐	☐	6.	☐	☐	7.	☐	☐	8.	☐	☐
9.	☐	☐	10.	☐	☐	11.	☐	☐	12.	☐	☐	13.	☐	☐	14.	☐	☐	15.	☐	☐	16.	☐	☐
17.	☐	☐	18.	☐	☐	19.	☐	☐	20.	☐	☐	21.	☐	☐	22.	☐	☐	23.	☐	☐	24.	☐	☐
25.	☐	☐	26.	☐	☐	27.	☐	☐	28.	☐	☐	29.	☐	☐	30.	☐	☐	31.	☐	☐	32.	☐	☐
33.	☐	☐	34.	☐	☐	35.	☐	☐	36.	☐	☐	37.	☐	☐	38.	☐	☐	39.	☐	☐	40.	☐	☐

	T	F		T	F		T	F		T	F		T	F		T	F		T	F		T	F
41.	☐	☐	42.	☐	☐	43.	☐	☐	44.	☐	☐	45.	☐	☐	46.	☐	☐	47.	☐	☐	48.	☐	☐
49.	☐	☐	50.	☐	☐	51.	☐	☐	52.	☐	☐	53.	☐	☐	54.	☐	☐	55.	☐	☐	56.	☐	☐
57.	☐	☐	58.	☐	☐	59.	☐	☐	60.	☐	☐	61.	☐	☐	62.	☐	☐	63.	☐	☐	64.	☐	☐
65.	☐	☐	66.	☐	☐	67.	☐	☐	68.	☐	☐	69.	☐	☐	70.	☐	☐	71.	☐	☐	72.	☐	☐
73.	☐	☐	74.	☐	☐	75.	☐	☐	76.	☐	☐	77.	☐	☐	78.	☐	☐	79.	☐	☐	80.	☐	☐

	T	F		T	F		T	F		T	F		T	F		T	F		T	F		T	F
81.	☐	☐	82.	☐	☐	83.	☐	☐	84.	☐	☐	85.	☐	☐	86.	☐	☐	87.	☐	☐	88.	☐	☐
89.	☐	☐	90.	☐	☐	91.	☐	☐	92.	☐	☐	93.	☐	☐	94.	☐	☐	95.	☐	☐	96.	☐	☐
97.	☐	☐	98.	☐	☐	99.	☐	☐	100.	☐	☐	101.	☐	☐	102.	☐	☐	103.	☐	☐	104.	☐	☐
105.	☐	☐	106.	☐	☐	107.	☐	☐	108.	☐	☐	109.	☐	☐	110.	☐	☐	111.	☐	☐	112.	☐	☐
113.	☐	☐	114.	☐	☐	115.	☐	☐	116.	☐	☐	117.	☐	☐	118.	☐	☐	119.	☐	☐	120.	☐	☐

THE MIND TEST

DIRECTIONS: Blacken in the boxes under T (True) or F (False) to show your response to each question.
Be careful to see that the number you mark is the same as the number of the question you are answering.

	T	F		T	F		T	F		T	F		T	F		T	F		T	F		T	F
1.	☐	☐	2.	☐	☐	3.	☐	☐	4.	☐	☐	5.	☐	☐	6.	☐	☐	7.	☐	☐	8.	☐	☐
9.	☐	☐	10.	☐	☐	11.	☐	☐	12.	☐	☐	13.	☐	☐	14.	☐	☐	15.	☐	☐	16.	☐	☐
17.	☐	☐	18.	☐	☐	19.	☐	☐	20.	☐	☐	21.	☐	☐	22.	☐	☐	23.	☐	☐	24.	☐	☐
25.	☐	☐	26.	☐	☐	27.	☐	☐	28.	☐	☐	29.	☐	☐	30.	☐	☐	31.	☐	☐	32.	☐	☐
33.	☐	☐	34.	☐	☐	35.	☐	☐	36.	☐	☐	37.	☐	☐	38.	☐	☐	39.	☐	☐	40.	☐	☐

	T	F		T	F		T	F		T	F		T	F		T	F		T	F		T	F
41.	☐	☐	42.	☐	☐	43.	☐	☐	44.	☐	☐	45.	☐	☐	46.	☐	☐	47.	☐	☐	48.	☐	☐
49.	☐	☐	50.	☐	☐	51.	☐	☐	52.	☐	☐	53.	☐	☐	54.	☐	☐	55.	☐	☐	56.	☐	☐
57.	☐	☐	58.	☐	☐	59.	☐	☐	60.	☐	☐	61.	☐	☐	62.	☐	☐	63.	☐	☐	64.	☐	☐
65.	☐	☐	66.	☐	☐	67.	☐	☐	68.	☐	☐	69.	☐	☐	70.	☐	☐	71.	☐	☐	72.	☐	☐
73.	☐	☐	74.	☐	☐	75.	☐	☐	76.	☐	☐	77.	☐	☐	78.	☐	☐	79.	☐	☐	80.	☐	☐

	T	F		T	F		T	F		T	F		T	F		T	F		T	F		T	F
81.	☐	☐	82.	☐	☐	83.	☐	☐	84.	☐	☐	85.	☐	☐	86.	☐	☐	87.	☐	☐	88.	☐	☐
89.	☐	☐	90.	☐	☐	91.	☐	☐	92.	☐	☐	93.	☐	☐	94.	☐	☐	95.	☐	☐	96.	☐	☐
97.	☐	☐	98.	☐	☐	99.	☐	☐	100.	☐	☐	101.	☐	☐	102.	☐	☐	103.	☐	☐	104.	☐	☐
105.	☐	☐	106.	☐	☐	107.	☐	☐	108.	☐	☐	109.	☐	☐	110.	☐	☐	111.	☐	☐	112.	☐	☐
113.	☐	☐	114.	☐	☐	115.	☐	☐	116.	☐	☐	117.	☐	☐	118.	☐	☐	119.	☐	☐	120.	☐	☐

THE
MIND TEST

DIRECTIONS: Blacken in the boxes under T (True) or F (False) to show your response to each question.
Be careful to see that the number you mark is the same as the number of the question you are answering.

	T F	T F	T F	T F	T F	T F	T F	T F
	1. ☐ ☐	2. ☐ ☐	3. ☐ ☐	4. ☐ ☐	5. ☐ ☐	6. ☐ ☐	7. ☐ ☐	8. ☐ ☐
	9. ☐ ☐	10. ☐ ☐	11. ☐ ☐	12. ☐ ☐	13. ☐ ☐	14. ☐ ☐	15. ☐ ☐	16. ☐ ☐
	17. ☐ ☐	18. ☐ ☐	19. ☐ ☐	20. ☐ ☐	21. ☐ ☐	22. ☐ ☐	23. ☐ ☐	24. ☐ ☐
	25. ☐ ☐	26. ☐ ☐	27. ☐ ☐	28. ☐ ☐	29. ☐ ☐	30. ☐ ☐	31. ☐ ☐	32. ☐ ☐
	33. ☐ ☐	34. ☐ ☐	35. ☐ ☐	36. ☐ ☐	37. ☐ ☐	38. ☐ ☐	39. ☐ ☐	40. ☐ ☐

	T F	T F	T F	T F	T F	T F	T F	T F
	41. ☐ ☐	42. ☐ ☐	43. ☐ ☐	44. ☐ ☐	45. ☐ ☐	46. ☐ ☐	47. ☐ ☐	48. ☐ ☐
	49. ☐ ☐	50. ☐ ☐	51. ☐ ☐	52. ☐ ☐	53. ☐ ☐	54. ☐ ☐	55. ☐ ☐	56. ☐ ☐
	57. ☐ ☐	58. ☐ ☐	59. ☐ ☐	60. ☐ ☐	61. ☐ ☐	62. ☐ ☐	63. ☐ ☐	64. ☐ ☐
	65. ☐ ☐	66. ☐ ☐	67. ☐ ☐	68. ☐ ☐	69. ☐ ☐	70. ☐ ☐	71. ☐ ☐	72. ☐ ☐
	73. ☐ ☐	74. ☐ ☐	75. ☐ ☐	76. ☐ ☐	77. ☐ ☐	78. ☐ ☐	79. ☐ ☐	80. ☐ ☐

	T F	T F	T F	T F	T F	T F	T F	T F
	81. ☐ ☐	82. ☐ ☐	83. ☐ ☐	84. ☐ ☐	85. ☐ ☐	86. ☐ ☐	87. ☐ ☐	88. ☐ ☐
	89. ☐ ☐	90. ☐ ☐	91. ☐ ☐	92. ☐ ☐	93. ☐ ☐	94. ☐ ☐	95. ☐ ☐	96. ☐ ☐
	97. ☐ ☐	98. ☐ ☐	99. ☐ ☐	100. ☐ ☐	101. ☐ ☐	102. ☐ ☐	103. ☐ ☐	104. ☐ ☐
	105. ☐ ☐	106. ☐ ☐	107. ☐ ☐	108. ☐ ☐	109. ☐ ☐	110. ☐ ☐	111. ☐ ☐	112. ☐ ☐
	113. ☐ ☐	114. ☐ ☐	115. ☐ ☐	116. ☐ ☐	117. ☐ ☐	118. ☐ ☐	119. ☐ ☐	120. ☐ ☐

THE MIND TEST

DIRECTIONS: Blacken in the boxes under T (True) or F (False) to show your response to each question. Be careful to see that the number you mark is the same as the number of the question you are answering.

T F	T F	T F	T F	T F	T F	T F	T F
1. ☐ ☐	2. ☐ ☐	3. ☐ ☐	4. ☐ ☐	5. ☐ ☐	6. ☐ ☐	7. ☐ ☐	8. ☐ ☐
9. ☐ ☐	10. ☐ ☐	11. ☐ ☐	12. ☐ ☐	13. ☐ ☐	14. ☐ ☐	15. ☐ ☐	16. ☐ ☐
17. ☐ ☐	18. ☐ ☐	19. ☐ ☐	20. ☐ ☐	21. ☐ ☐	22. ☐ ☐	23. ☐ ☐	24. ☐ ☐
25. ☐ ☐	26. ☐ ☐	27. ☐ ☐	28. ☐ ☐	29. ☐ ☐	30. ☐ ☐	31. ☐ ☐	32. ☐ ☐
33. ☐ ☐	34. ☐ ☐	35. ☐ ☐	36. ☐ ☐	37. ☐ ☐	38. ☐ ☐	39. ☐ ☐	40. ☐ ☐

T F	T F	T F	T F	T F	T F	T F	T F
41. ☐ ☐	42. ☐ ☐	43. ☐ ☐	44. ☐ ☐	45. ☐ ☐	46. ☐ ☐	47. ☐ ☐	48. ☐ ☐
49. ☐ ☐	50. ☐ ☐	51. ☐ ☐	52. ☐ ☐	53. ☐ ☐	54. ☐ ☐	55. ☐ ☐	56. ☐ ☐
57. ☐ ☐	58. ☐ ☐	59. ☐ ☐	60. ☐ ☐	61. ☐ ☐	62. ☐ ☐	63. ☐ ☐	64. ☐ ☐
65. ☐ ☐	66. ☐ ☐	67. ☐ ☐	68. ☐ ☐	69. ☐ ☐	70. ☐ ☐	71. ☐ ☐	72. ☐ ☐
73. ☐ ☐	74. ☐ ☐	75. ☐ ☐	76. ☐ ☐	77. ☐ ☐	78. ☐ ☐	79. ☐ ☐	80. ☐ ☐

T F	T F	T F	T F	T F	T F	T F	T F
81. ☐ ☐	82. ☐ ☐	83. ☐ ☐	84. ☐ ☐	85. ☐ ☐	86. ☐ ☐	87. ☐ ☐	88. ☐ ☐
89. ☐ ☐	90. ☐ ☐	91. ☐ ☐	92. ☐ ☐	93. ☐ ☐	94. ☐ ☐	95. ☐ ☐	96. ☐ ☐
97. ☐ ☐	98. ☐ ☐	99. ☐ ☐	100. ☐ ☐	101. ☐ ☐	102. ☐ ☐	103. ☐ ☐	104. ☐ ☐
105. ☐ ☐	106. ☐ ☐	107. ☐ ☐	108. ☐ ☐	109. ☐ ☐	110. ☐ ☐	111. ☐ ☐	112. ☐ ☐
113. ☐ ☐	114. ☐ ☐	115. ☐ ☐	116. ☐ ☐	117. ☐ ☐	118. ☐ ☐	119. ☐ ☐	120. ☐ ☐

THE MIND TEST

DIRECTIONS: Blacken in the boxes under T (True) or F (False) to show your response to each question.

Be careful to see that the number you mark is the same as the number of the question you are answering.

	T	F		T	F		T	F		T	F		T	F		T	F		T	F		T	F
1.	☐	☐	2.	☐	☐	3.	☐	☐	4.	☐	☐	5.	☐	☐	6.	☐	☐	7.	☐	☐	8.	☐	☐
9.	☐	☐	10.	☐	☐	11.	☐	☐	12.	☐	☐	13.	☐	☐	14.	☐	☐	15.	☐	☐	16.	☐	☐
17.	☐	☐	18.	☐	☐	19.	☐	☐	20.	☐	☐	21.	☐	☐	22.	☐	☐	23.	☐	☐	24.	☐	☐
25.	☐	☐	26.	☐	☐	27.	☐	☐	28.	☐	☐	29.	☐	☐	30.	☐	☐	31.	☐	☐	32.	☐	☐
33.	☐	☐	34.	☐	☐	35.	☐	☐	36.	☐	☐	37.	☐	☐	38.	☐	☐	39.	☐	☐	40.	☐	☐

	T	F		T	F		T	F		T	F		T	F		T	F		T	F		T	F
41.	☐	☐	42.	☐	☐	43.	☐	☐	44.	☐	☐	45.	☐	☐	46.	☐	☐	47.	☐	☐	48.	☐	☐
49.	☐	☐	50.	☐	☐	51.	☐	☐	52.	☐	☐	53.	☐	☐	54.	☐	☐	55.	☐	☐	56.	☐	☐
57.	☐	☐	58.	☐	☐	59.	☐	☐	60.	☐	☐	61.	☐	☐	62.	☐	☐	63.	☐	☐	64.	☐	☐
65.	☐	☐	66.	☐	☐	67.	☐	☐	68.	☐	☐	69.	☐	☐	70.	☐	☐	71.	☐	☐	72.	☐	☐
73.	☐	☐	74.	☐	☐	75.	☐	☐	76.	☐	☐	77.	☐	☐	78.	☐	☐	79.	☐	☐	80.	☐	☐

	T	F		T	F		T	F		T	F		T	F		T	F		T	F		T	F
81.	☐	☐	82.	☐	☐	83.	☐	☐	84.	☐	☐	85.	☐	☐	86.	☐	☐	87.	☐	☐	88.	☐	☐
89.	☐	☐	90.	☐	☐	91.	☐	☐	92.	☐	☐	93.	☐	☐	94.	☐	☐	95.	☐	☐	96.	☐	☐
97.	☐	☐	98.	☐	☐	99.	☐	☐	100.	☐	☐	101.	☐	☐	102.	☐	☐	103.	☐	☐	104.	☐	☐
105.	☐	☐	106.	☐	☐	107.	☐	☐	108.	☐	☐	109.	☐	☐	110.	☐	☐	111.	☐	☐	112.	☐	☐
113.	☐	☐	114.	☐	☐	115.	☐	☐	116.	☐	☐	117.	☐	☐	118.	☐	☐	119.	☐	☐	120.	☐	☐

THE MIND TEST

DIRECTIONS: Blacken in the boxes under T (True) or F (False) to show your response to each question.

Be careful to see that the number you mark is the same as the number of the question you are answering.

	T	F		T	F		T	F		T	F		T	F		T	F		T	F		T	F
1.	☐	☐	2.	☐	☐	3.	☐	☐	4.	☐	☐	5.	☐	☐	6.	☐	☐	7.	☐	☐	8.	☐	☐
9.	☐	☐	10.	☐	☐	11.	☐	☐	12.	☐	☐	13.	☐	☐	14.	☐	☐	15.	☐	☐	16.	☐	☐
17.	☐	☐	18.	☐	☐	19.	☐	☐	20.	☐	☐	21.	☐	☐	22.	☐	☐	23.	☐	☐	24.	☐	☐
25.	☐	☐	26.	☐	☐	27.	☐	☐	28.	☐	☐	29.	☐	☐	30.	☐	☐	31.	☐	☐	32.	☐	☐
33.	☐	☐	34.	☐	☐	35.	☐	☐	36.	☐	☐	37.	☐	☐	38.	☐	☐	39.	☐	☐	40.	☐	☐

	T	F		T	F		T	F		T	F		T	F		T	F		T	F		T	F
41.	☐	☐	42.	☐	☐	43.	☐	☐	44.	☐	☐	45.	☐	☐	46.	☐	☐	47.	☐	☐	48.	☐	☐
49.	☐	☐	50.	☐	☐	51.	☐	☐	52.	☐	☐	53.	☐	☐	54.	☐	☐	55.	☐	☐	56.	☐	☐
57.	☐	☐	58.	☐	☐	59.	☐	☐	60.	☐	☐	61.	☐	☐	62.	☐	☐	63.	☐	☐	64.	☐	☐
65.	☐	☐	66.	☐	☐	67.	☐	☐	68.	☐	☐	69.	☐	☐	70.	☐	☐	71.	☐	☐	72.	☐	☐
73.	☐	☐	74.	☐	☐	75.	☐	☐	76.	☐	☐	77.	☐	☐	78.	☐	☐	79.	☐	☐	80.	☐	☐

	T	F		T	F		T	F		T	F		T	F		T	F		T	F		T	F
81.	☐	☐	82.	☐	☐	83.	☐	☐	84.	☐	☐	85.	☐	☐	86.	☐	☐	87.	☐	☐	88.	☐	☐
89.	☐	☐	90.	☐	☐	91.	☐	☐	92.	☐	☐	93.	☐	☐	94.	☐	☐	95.	☐	☐	96.	☐	☐
97.	☐	☐	98.	☐	☐	99.	☐	☐	100.	☐	☐	101.	☐	☐	102.	☐	☐	103.	☐	☐	104.	☐	☐
105.	☐	☐	106.	☐	☐	107.	☐	☐	108.	☐	☐	109.	☐	☐	110.	☐	☐	111.	☐	☐	112.	☐	☐
113.	☐	☐	114.	☐	☐	115.	☐	☐	116.	☐	☐	117.	☐	☐	118.	☐	☐	119.	☐	☐	120.	☐	☐

THE MIND TEST

DIRECTIONS: Blacken in the boxes under T (True) or F (False) to show your response to each question. Be careful to see that the number you mark is the same as the number of the question you are answering.

	T	F		T	F		T	F		T	F		T	F		T	F		T	F		T	F
1.	☐	☐	2.	☐	☐	3.	☐	☐	4.	☐	☐	5.	☐	☐	6.	☐	☐	7.	☐	☐	8.	☐	☐
9.	☐	☐	10.	☐	☐	11.	☐	☐	12.	☐	☐	13.	☐	☐	14.	☐	☐	15.	☐	☐	16.	☐	☐
17.	☐	☐	18.	☐	☐	19.	☐	☐	20.	☐	☐	21.	☐	☐	22.	☐	☐	23.	☐	☐	24.	☐	☐
25.	☐	☐	26.	☐	☐	27.	☐	☐	28.	☐	☐	29.	☐	☐	30.	☐	☐	31.	☐	☐	32.	☐	☐
33.	☐	☐	34.	☐	☐	35.	☐	☐	36.	☐	☐	37.	☐	☐	38.	☐	☐	39.	☐	☐	40.	☐	☐

	T	F		T	F		T	F		T	F		T	F		T	F		T	F		T	F
41.	☐	☐	42.	☐	☐	43.	☐	☐	44.	☐	☐	45.	☐	☐	46.	☐	☐	47.	☐	☐	48.	☐	☐
49.	☐	☐	50.	☐	☐	51.	☐	☐	52.	☐	☐	53.	☐	☐	54.	☐	☐	55.	☐	☐	56.	☐	☐
57.	☐	☐	58.	☐	☐	59.	☐	☐	60.	☐	☐	61.	☐	☐	62.	☐	☐	63.	☐	☐	64.	☐	☐
65.	☐	☐	66.	☐	☐	67.	☐	☐	68.	☐	☐	69.	☐	☐	70.	☐	☐	71.	☐	☐	72.	☐	☐
73.	☐	☐	74.	☐	☐	75.	☐	☐	76.	☐	☐	77.	☐	☐	78.	☐	☐	79.	☐	☐	80.	☐	☐

	T	F		T	F		T	F		T	F		T	F		T	F		T	F		T	F
81.	☐	☐	82.	☐	☐	83.	☐	☐	84.	☐	☐	85.	☐	☐	86.	☐	☐	87.	☐	☐	88.	☐	☐
89.	☐	☐	90.	☐	☐	91.	☐	☐	92.	☐	☐	93.	☐	☐	94.	☐	☐	95.	☐	☐	96.	☐	☐
97.	☐	☐	98.	☐	☐	99.	☐	☐	100.	☐	☐	101.	☐	☐	102.	☐	☐	103.	☐	☐	104.	☐	☐
105.	☐	☐	106.	☐	☐	107.	☐	☐	108.	☐	☐	109.	☐	☐	110.	☐	☐	111.	☐	☐	112.	☐	☐
113.	☐	☐	114.	☐	☐	115.	☐	☐	116.	☐	☐	117.	☐	☐	118.	☐	☐	119.	☐	☐	120.	☐	☐

THE MIND TEST

DIRECTIONS: Blacken in the boxes under T (True) or F (False) to show your response to each question. Be careful to see that the number you mark is the same as the number of the question you are answering.

T	F		T	F		T	F		T	F		T	F		T	F		T	F		T	F
1. ☐	☐	2. ☐	☐	3. ☐	☐	4. ☐	☐	5. ☐	☐	6. ☐	☐	7. ☐	☐	8. ☐	☐
9. ☐	☐	10. ☐	☐	11. ☐	☐	12. ☐	☐	13. ☐	☐	14. ☐	☐	15. ☐	☐	16. ☐	☐
17. ☐	☐	18. ☐	☐	19. ☐	☐	20. ☐	☐	21. ☐	☐	22. ☐	☐	23. ☐	☐	24. ☐	☐
25. ☐	☐	26. ☐	☐	27. ☐	☐	28. ☐	☐	29. ☐	☐	30. ☐	☐	31. ☐	☐	32. ☐	☐
33. ☐	☐	34. ☐	☐	35. ☐	☐	36. ☐	☐	37. ☐	☐	38. ☐	☐	39. ☐	☐	40. ☐	☐

T	F		T	F		T	F		T	F		T	F		T	F		T	F		T	F
41. ☐	☐	42. ☐	☐	43. ☐	☐	44. ☐	☐	45. ☐	☐	46. ☐	☐	47. ☐	☐	48. ☐	☐
49. ☐	☐	50. ☐	☐	51. ☐	☐	52. ☐	☐	53. ☐	☐	54. ☐	☐	55. ☐	☐	56. ☐	☐
57. ☐	☐	58. ☐	☐	59. ☐	☐	60. ☐	☐	61. ☐	☐	62. ☐	☐	63. ☐	☐	64. ☐	☐
65. ☐	☐	66. ☐	☐	67. ☐	☐	68. ☐	☐	69. ☐	☐	70. ☐	☐	71. ☐	☐	72. ☐	☐
73. ☐	☐	74. ☐	☐	75. ☐	☐	76. ☐	☐	77. ☐	☐	78. ☐	☐	79. ☐	☐	80. ☐	☐

T	F		T	F		T	F		T	F		T	F		T	F		T	F		T	F
81. ☐	☐	82. ☐	☐	83. ☐	☐	84. ☐	☐	85. ☐	☐	86. ☐	☐	87. ☐	☐	88. ☐	☐
89. ☐	☐	90. ☐	☐	91. ☐	☐	92. ☐	☐	93. ☐	☐	94. ☐	☐	95. ☐	☐	96. ☐	☐
97. ☐	☐	98. ☐	☐	99. ☐	☐	100. ☐	☐	101. ☐	☐	102. ☐	☐	103. ☐	☐	104. ☐	☐
105. ☐	☐	106. ☐	☐	107. ☐	☐	108. ☐	☐	109. ☐	☐	110. ☐	☐	111. ☐	☐	112. ☐	☐
113. ☐	☐	114. ☐	☐	115. ☐	☐	116. ☐	☐	117. ☐	☐	118. ☐	☐	119. ☐	☐	120. ☐	☐

THE MIND TEST

DIRECTIONS: Blacken in the boxes under T (True) or F (False) to show your response to each question. Be careful to see that the number you mark is the same as the number of the question you are answering.

	T	F		T	F		T	F		T	F		T	F		T	F		T	F		T	F
1.	□	□	2.	□	□	3.	□	□	4.	□	□	5.	□	□	6.	□	□	7.	□	□	8.	□	□
9.	□	□	10.	□	□	11.	□	□	12.	□	□	13.	□	□	14.	□	□	15.	□	□	16.	□	□
17.	□	□	18.	□	□	19.	□	□	20.	□	□	21.	□	□	22.	□	□	23.	□	□	24.	□	□
25.	□	□	26.	□	□	27.	□	□	28.	□	□	29.	□	□	30.	□	□	31.	□	□	32.	□	□
33.	□	□	34.	□	□	35.	□	□	36.	□	□	37.	□	□	38.	□	□	39.	□	□	40.	□	□

	T	F		T	F		T	F		T	F		T	F		T	F		T	F		T	F
41.	□	□	42.	□	□	43.	□	□	44.	□	□	45.	□	□	46.	□	□	47.	□	□	48.	□	□
49.	□	□	50.	□	□	51.	□	□	52.	□	□	53.	□	□	54.	□	□	55.	□	□	56.	□	□
57.	□	□	58.	□	□	59.	□	□	60.	□	□	61.	□	□	62.	□	□	63.	□	□	64.	□	□
65.	□	□	66.	□	□	67.	□	□	68.	□	□	69.	□	□	70.	□	□	71.	□	□	72.	□	□
73.	□	□	74.	□	□	75.	□	□	76.	□	□	77.	□	□	78.	□	□	79.	□	□	80.	□	□

	T	F		T	F		T	F		T	F		T	F		T	F		T	F		T	F
81.	□	□	82.	□	□	83.	□	□	84.	□	□	85.	□	□	86.	□	□	87.	□	□	88.	□	□
89.	□	□	90.	□	□	91.	□	□	92.	□	□	93.	□	□	94.	□	□	95.	□	□	96.	□	□
97.	□	□	98.	□	□	99.	□	□	100.	□	□	101.	□	□	102.	□	□	103.	□	□	104.	□	□
105.	□	□	106.	□	□	107.	□	□	108.	□	□	109.	□	□	110.	□	□	111.	□	□	112.	□	□
113.	□	□	114.	□	□	115.	□	□	116.	□	□	117.	□	□	118.	□	□	119.	□	□	120.	□	□

THE MIND TEST

DIRECTIONS: Blacken in the boxes under T (True) or F (False) to show your response to each question.

Be careful to see that the number you mark is the same as the number of the question you are answering.

	T	F		T	F		T	F		T	F		T	F		T	F		T	F		T	F
1.	☐	☐	2.	☐	☐	3.	☐	☐	4.	☐	☐	5.	☐	☐	6.	☐	☐	7.	☐	☐	8.	☐	☐
9.	☐	☐	10.	☐	☐	11.	☐	☐	12.	☐	☐	13.	☐	☐	14.	☐	☐	15.	☐	☐	16.	☐	☐
17.	☐	☐	18.	☐	☐	19.	☐	☐	20.	☐	☐	21.	☐	☐	22.	☐	☐	23.	☐	☐	24.	☐	☐
25.	☐	☐	26.	☐	☐	27.	☐	☐	28.	☐	☐	29.	☐	☐	30.	☐	☐	31.	☐	☐	32.	☐	☐
33.	☐	☐	34.	☐	☐	35.	☐	☐	36.	☐	☐	37.	☐	☐	38.	☐	☐	39.	☐	☐	40.	☐	☐

	T	F		T	F		T	F		T	F		T	F		T	F		T	F		T	F
41.	☐	☐	42.	☐	☐	43.	☐	☐	44.	☐	☐	45.	☐	☐	46.	☐	☐	47.	☐	☐	48.	☐	☐
49.	☐	☐	50.	☐	☐	51.	☐	☐	52.	☐	☐	53.	☐	☐	54.	☐	☐	55.	☐	☐	56.	☐	☐
57.	☐	☐	58.	☐	☐	59.	☐	☐	60.	☐	☐	61.	☐	☐	62.	☐	☐	63.	☐	☐	64.	☐	☐
65.	☐	☐	66.	☐	☐	67.	☐	☐	68.	☐	☐	69.	☐	☐	70.	☐	☐	71.	☐	☐	72.	☐	☐
73.	☐	☐	74.	☐	☐	75.	☐	☐	76.	☐	☐	77.	☐	☐	78.	☐	☐	79.	☐	☐	80.	☐	☐

	T	F		T	F		T	F		T	F		T	F		T	F		T	F		T	F
81.	☐	☐	82.	☐	☐	83.	☐	☐	84.	☐	☐	85.	☐	☐	86.	☐	☐	87.	☐	☐	88.	☐	☐
89.	☐	☐	90.	☐	☐	91.	☐	☐	92.	☐	☐	93.	☐	☐	94.	☐	☐	95.	☐	☐	96.	☐	☐
97.	☐	☐	98.	☐	☐	99.	☐	☐	100.	☐	☐	101.	☐	☐	102.	☐	☐	103.	☐	☐	104.	☐	☐
105.	☐	☐	106.	☐	☐	107.	☐	☐	108.	☐	☐	109.	☐	☐	110.	☐	☐	111.	☐	☐	112.	☐	☐
113.	☐	☐	114.	☐	☐	115.	☐	☐	116.	☐	☐	117.	☐	☐	118.	☐	☐	119.	☐	☐	120.	☐	☐

THE MIND TEST

DIRECTIONS: Blacken in the boxes under T (True) or F (False) to show your response to each question.

Be careful to see that the number you mark is the same as the number of the question you are answering.

T	F		T	F		T	F		T	F		T	F		T	F		T	F		T	F
1. ☐	☐	2. ☐	☐	3. ☐	☐	4. ☐	☐	5. ☐	☐	6. ☐	☐	7. ☐	☐	8. ☐	☐
9. ☐	☐	10. ☐	☐	11. ☐	☐	12. ☐	☐	13. ☐	☐	14. ☐	☐	15. ☐	☐	16. ☐	☐
17. ☐	☐	18. ☐	☐	19. ☐	☐	20. ☐	☐	21. ☐	☐	22. ☐	☐	23. ☐	☐	24. ☐	☐
25. ☐	☐	26. ☐	☐	27. ☐	☐	28. ☐	☐	29. ☐	☐	30. ☐	☐	31. ☐	☐	32. ☐	☐
33. ☐	☐	34. ☐	☐	35. ☐	☐	36. ☐	☐	37. ☐	☐	38. ☐	☐	39. ☐	☐	40. ☐	☐

T	F		T	F		T	F		T	F		T	F		T	F		T	F		T	F
41. ☐	☐	42. ☐	☐	43. ☐	☐	44. ☐	☐	45. ☐	☐	46. ☐	☐	47. ☐	☐	48. ☐	☐
49. ☐	☐	50. ☐	☐	51. ☐	☐	52. ☐	☐	53. ☐	☐	54. ☐	☐	55. ☐	☐	56. ☐	☐
57. ☐	☐	58. ☐	☐	59. ☐	☐	60. ☐	☐	61. ☐	☐	62. ☐	☐	63. ☐	☐	64. ☐	☐
65. ☐	☐	66. ☐	☐	67. ☐	☐	68. ☐	☐	69. ☐	☐	70. ☐	☐	71. ☐	☐	72. ☐	☐
73. ☐	☐	74. ☐	☐	75. ☐	☐	76. ☐	☐	77. ☐	☐	78. ☐	☐	79. ☐	☐	80. ☐	☐

T	F		T	F		T	F		T	F		T	F		T	F		T	F		T	F
81. ☐	☐	82. ☐	☐	83. ☐	☐	84. ☐	☐	85. ☐	☐	86. ☐	☐	87. ☐	☐	88. ☐	☐
89. ☐	☐	90. ☐	☐	91. ☐	☐	92. ☐	☐	93. ☐	☐	94. ☐	☐	95. ☐	☐	96. ☐	☐
97. ☐	☐	98. ☐	☐	99. ☐	☐	100. ☐	☐	101. ☐	☐	102. ☐	☐	103. ☐	☐	104. ☐	☐
105. ☐	☐	106. ☐	☐	107. ☐	☐	108. ☐	☐	109. ☐	☐	110. ☐	☐	111. ☐	☐	112. ☐	☐
113. ☐	☐	114. ☐	☐	115. ☐	☐	116. ☐	☐	117. ☐	☐	118. ☐	☐	119. ☐	☐	120. ☐	☐